CIVIL RIGHTS IN

SOUTH CAROLINA

From Peaceful Protests to Groundbreaking Rulings

JAMES L. FELDER

THE
History
PRESS

Published by The History Press
Charleston, SC 29403
www.historypress.net

Copyright © 2012 by James L. Felder
All rights reserved

First published 2012
Second printing 2012

Manufactured in the United States

ISBN 978.1.60949.686.9

Library of Congress CIP data applied for.

Dedicated to my children and grandchildren.

My legacy to you is to know your history.

CONTENTS

Contents

ACKNOWLEDGEMENTS

Thanks to the late Judge Matthew J. Perry, who at the dedication of the federal courthouse that bears his name urged me to tell the story of the unsung foot soldiers of the civil rights movement in South Carolina. I regret that he is not here to see the finished product.

To the mother of my children, Charletta P. Felder, thanks for reviewing the manuscript and preparing the table of contents.

To my children, Jimmy and Adrienne, who kept asking, "Dad, when are you going to finish the book?" Your asking pushed me to complete it.

Thanks to Gwen Foushe, the administrative assistant to one of my mentors, senator and reverend I.D. Nwewman, for reviewing the first chapter and providing information on the senator.

Thanks to Jessica Berzon and Jaime Muehl of The History Press for expediting the process of this book so that I could meet my deadline for releasing it.

INTRODUCTION

The idea to write this book came to me in 1973. My first thought was to do a period piece, from 1954 to 1974, covering the changes that had occurred in the black community of South Carolina since the historic *Brown v. Board of Education* ruling. After conducting some 112 interviews with elders in the black community who were intimately involved in the shaping of the changes, I put the information aside because of some personal setbacks that I had to deal with at the time.

I did not revive this project until the mid-1980s, after having spent two years as executive vice-president of Operation PUSH and traveling inside and outside of this country with longtime friend and fraternity brother Reverend Jesse L. Jackson Sr. That experience itself is worthy of writing about, and I plan to do so upon completion of this book. I decided to expand the period of coverage and move the starting point back to 1939. That year was a turning point in history, both nationally and internationally, because of Germany's invasion of Poland, which triggered World War II. However, the big event in the black community of South Carolina in 1939 was the founding of the South Carolina Conference of Branches NAACP. This event marked the beginning of the fight for civil rights gains in the state.

The purpose of this book is to provide accurate and comprehensive coverage of the period. Drawing on in-depth interviews, newspaper reports and my own personal observations and experiences, I have tried to paint a picture of the movers and shakers and events of the period that will be informative and educational for readers, young and old, black and white.

INTRODUCTION

The NAACP was the vehicle most commonly used in South Carolina to secure civil rights for people of color. Therefore, this book in many ways will be a history of the South Carolina Conference of Branches NAACP. Yes, there were other organizations and groups in the struggle for justice and equality in South Carolina, and they will be recognized. However, by and large, it was the NAACP that followed through and made things happen.

The difficulty in writing this book was trying to be objective and detached. I was fortunate to have known and met 95 percent of the movers and shakers you will read about, plus I scored a few firsts myself. There were times when it was difficult trying to stay in a narrative history mode and not slip into autobiographical or memoir mode.

The other reason for writing this book was to highlight and showcase the many unsung, unheard-of and/or forgotten heroes and heroines who took great risks, sacrificed much and dared to challenge the segregated establishment and right the wrongs of the times. The "classic example" was John H. Wrighten III, a World War II veteran who wanted to attend law school at the University of South Carolina since it was the only one in the state. Because the law school was closed to blacks, Wrighten had to sue the university board of trustees for admission. The result was that the South Carolina legislature appropriated funds to build a law school and medical school at South Carolina State College, the segregated black public school of higher education at the time. Along with Wrighten, South Carolina State Law School produced some of the legal giants of color in this state. They include Judge Matthew J. Perry of the United States District Court, Chief Justice Ernest A. Finney Jr. of the South Carolina Supreme Court, Judge Jasper M. Cureton of the South Carolina Court of Appeals, Judge Danny Martin of the South Carolina Circuit Court and Judges Willie T. Smith and Ruben Gray of the South Carolina Family Court.

Another classic example of unsung heroines is Sarah Mae Flemming of Eastover, South Carolina. Most people date the modern civil rights movement to Dr. Martin Luther King Jr. and the Montgomery, Alabama bus boycott wherein Rosa Parks refused to give up *her* seat in the "white-only" section of the bus on December 1, 1955. However, a full year and a half before that incident, on June 24, 1954, Flemming refused to give up *her* seat on a South Carolina Electric & Gas bus in Columbia, and after an altercation with the driver, she sued and won the right to sit at the front of bus. When the Parks case reached the U.S. Supreme Court, it refused to hear it, saying the court had acted on a similar matter in the Flemming case, and Montgomery had to desegregate its buses.

And of course there were the dirt farmers of Clarendon County who had the audacity to put their names on petitions for better schools in the historic *Briggs v. Elliott* lawsuit that joined four other pieces of litigation that reached the U.S. Supreme Court and became the landmark case known as *Brown v. Board of Education*. The plaintiffs in these cases are all highlighted in this book.

There is a common thread that runs through most of the lawsuits of this era. That thread was Judge J. Waties Waring, a white Charleston aristocrat who, as a U.S. Federal District Court judge, presided over most of the litigation. There is no doubt that without his presence in the equation, simple justice would have been denied to South Carolina citizens of color for a much longer period.

It was for all of the above reasons that I decided to chronicle the events of the period from 1939 to 2011 so that they can be preserved for my children and posterity.

1

A PLUMBER AND A MAILMAN

Levi G. Byrd, a plumber from Cheraw, and S.J. McDonald Sr., a railway mail clerk from Sumter, teamed up to issue a call for organizing the NAACP branches in South Carolina into what would become a statewide organization called the South Carolina Conference of Branches NAACP. Representatives from eight of the existing nine branches attended that October 15, 1939 meeting, which was held in the basement of the library at Benedict College in Columbia. Those branches were Aiken, Charleston, Cheraw, Florence, Georgetown, Greenville, Rock Hill and Sumter. The ninth branch, Columbia, joined a year later. It is reported that the Columbia branch did not attend because it was not included in the initial planning and therefore was pouting.

The NAACP was founded in 1909 in New York by W.E.B. DuBois, Ida B. Wells and several Jewish residents. It would become *the* civil rights organization of the century and continues to this day. There were chapters—or, as they are sometimes called, branches—throughout the United States. However, they all were autonomous bodies, and each could elect to pursue whatever civil rights activities it so desired.

This effort by Byrd and McDonald to organize the South Carolina branches would be the beginning of the struggle for active civil and legal rights in South Carolina. The officers elected at this first meeting were: Reverend A.W. Wright of Cheraw, president; Reverend H.W.D. Stewart of Greenville and W.N. Roseborough of Columbia, vice-presidents; Bernice Robinson of Cheraw, secretary; Anna Daniels Reuben of Georgetown, assistant secretary; Levi G. Byrd of Cheraw, treasurer; S.J. McDonald

Sr. of Sumter, chair of the executive committee; and Modjeska Simkins of Columbia, executive committee. In spite of the Columbia Branch's reluctance to attend this meeting, Simkins attended anyway, which act began a lifetime career of civil rights activity by this grand lady.

Byrd moved to South Carolina from North Carolina in 1927, seeking employment. He was an unlettered man and worked as a plumber's assistant. By 1931, he was the only plumber working in Cheraw. He never learned to drive a car, so he carried his tools on his bicycle. His involvement in civil rights grew out of a beating he took at the hands of the Ku Klux Klan, which ridiculed him about his lack of education. This drove him to immerse himself in NAACP activities for the rest of his life. Whites in Cheraw tolerated his NAACP activities because he was the only plumber in town.

In 1971, in an effort to honor Byrd for his years of struggles, Roy Wilkins, executive secretary of the NAACP, came to a program in Cheraw celebrating Byrd's work. It was truly a noteworthy occasion because it brought in luminaries and dignitaries from all over South Carolina to recognize this humble man. During his many years of service as treasurer of the state NAACP, Byrd rode the Greyhound bus from Cheraw to Columbia for the monthly meetings. Byrd died in 1985 while serving as treasurer emeritus of the South Carolina Conference NAACP. His picture hangs on the wall in the State Conference Office in Columbia. In 2008, a park was named in his honor, located at 107 Church Street in Cheraw.

Byrd's partner in this effort to organize this statewide NAACP organization was S.J. McDonald Sr. McDonald was born in Lynchburg, South Carolina, a small rural community just outside Sumter. He attended Claflin University in Orangeburg and became a teacher in the rural schools of Sumter County. He gave up teaching and became a railway mail clerk, a position he held for thirty-four years. This position guaranteed him the security he needed as he ventured into these NAACP and civil rights activities. McDonald was the co-organizer of the Sumter Branch NAACP. He served for twelve years as chair of the state NAACP organization.

As a member of Emmanuel United Methodist Church in Sumter, he was very active in the district and national affairs of the Methodist Church. For twenty-four consecutive years, McDonald served as a delegate from the South Carolina Methodist Conference to the Central Jurisdiction of the Methodist Church. In those days, all black Methodists were in one conference. It did not matter whether you lived in New York, Arkansas or Florida; if you were black, you belonged to the Central Jurisdiction of the Methodist Church. This would change in 1968, when the Methodists merged all of their conferences and became the United Methodist Church. The first experiment to come out of that merger was to assign a black Sumter native, Bishop James Thomas, to a 98 percent white conference in Iowa. In 1996, South Carolina would receive its first black bishop, Joseph Bethea, a Claflin University graduate.

McDonald was very productive. He was the father of six children, and apparently medicine was in his DNA. Four of his children and two of his grandsons entered the medical profession. S.J. McDonald Jr., Bruce McDonald and Harry McDonald all became physicians. Edmond "Buck" McDonald became a dentist, and his son, Edmond McDonald Jr., pursued a dental career as well. Renard, the son of S.J. McDonald Jr., became a physician.

Mr. McDonald would sit on his front porch with grandson Renard and observe the Ku Klux Klan parade past his home on West Oakland Avenue in Sumter. He never feared the Klan and told his grandson not to fear it either. Morris College in Sumter bestowed on McDonald an honorary doctorate of humanities degree for his services to the Sumter Branch NAACP and the state NAACP. He was married to Adelaide Palmer of Columbia. Mrs. McDonald's father, Robert J. Palmer, served in the South Carolina House of Representatives during Reconstruction from 1876 to 1878.

On Friday, October 12, 2007, the South Carolina Voter Education Project honored McDonald as its Trail Blazer awardee posthumously. The speaker for the occasion was former first lady and U.S. senator Hillary Rodham Clinton. The affair was held at the Brookland Banquet and Convention Center in West Columbia and attended by more than seven hundred people. His last living son, Dr. Harry McDonald, grandchildren and great-grandchildren attended the event. McDonald died on January 12, 1968.

WHO WERE THE OTHER PERSONS willing to put their lives and fortunes on the line for this organization that was so hated by the KKK and most whites in the state at that time? It was called the NAACP, but to most whites, it was called "trouble."

The new president, Reverend A.W. Wright, was a pastor in Cheraw and the spiritual leader of Levi G. Byrd. W.N. Roseboro, vice-president, was the executive of the Prince Hall Masonic Temple in Columbia and served as poll manager for the Ward Nine Precinct.

The secretary, Bernice-Stokes Robinson, was born in Sumter and was the youngest of eleven children of the Reverend Rufus E. Stokes. Upon the passing of her mother, Reverend Stokes allowed a cousin to serve as guardian for the young Bernice. At age thirteen, she enrolled in Coulter Academy in Cheraw. Coulter was a school established in 1881 by the Presbyterian Church to educate blacks in Chesterfield County because they could not attend the white public schools. Upon graduation, Robinson took correspondence courses from South Carolina State College, Alabama State and A&T State College. In 1950, she graduated summa cum laude from Barber-Scotia College in Concord, North Carolina. Mrs. Robinson taught in the Chesterfield County schools for forty-one years. Upon retirement, she transitioned into operating a nursery and kindergarten and writing a weekly column for the *Cheraw Chronicle* that highlighted the people and events in the black community of Chesterfield County.

Anna Daniels Reuben, the assistant secretary, was a native of Georgetown, South Carolina. She married Dr. O.R. Reuben, who later became president of Morris College in Sumter. She earned a PhD and taught at the college until her retirement. In 1969, Governor Robert E. McNair appointed her to the South Carolina Department of After Care board, a first for blacks in the state.

Modjeska Simkins, who was elected to the executive board, was a Columbia native. She attended grade school and high school on the campus of Benedict College and received a bachelor's of art degree from Benedict in 1921. She began teaching at Booker T. Washington High School that same year. Because public schools in South Carolina did not allow married women to teach, she was asked to resign when she married Andrew Simkins in 1929. Shortly after that, she was hired as director of the South Carolina Tuberculosis Association's Negro Work Program, a position that lasted until 1942. She was released due to her participation in civil rights activities. She hosted a weekly program on WOIC Radio Station in Columbia and started each program by saying, "I woke up this morning with freedom on my mind." She headed many voter registration drives in Columbia. Her family-owned bank, Victory Savings Bank, had a branch on Harden Street across from Allen University and Benedict College that she managed. It was there that she registered students from the colleges to vote and gave them real-life civic lessons on participation in the political process.

Simkins was truly a lightning rod who went after racism and disparities in this state. She was active in the Democratic Party, both state and national. Her home was a bed-and-breakfast for Thurgood Marshall and his legal team when they visited South Carolina. She helped draft many of the petitions seeking desegregation in the schools and other projects. She edited a newsletter for the Citizen Committee. In 1941, she was elected secretary of the State Conference NAACP, a position she held until 1957. Her work helped the state move toward racial quality. Her home on Marion Street in Columbia is now a museum for civil rights exhibits and other community activities. She died in 1992 at the age of ninety-seven. Her funeral was held on the campus of Benedict College. In attendance was a person with whom she did not always agree: former governor Robert E. McNair. A portrait of Modjeska Simkins now hangs in the South Carolina Statehouse (see chapter twenty for more details on portraits).

A YEAR AND A HALF following the organization of the State Conference NAACP, some changes would occur. In 1941, Reverend J.M. Hinton of Columbia was elected State Conference president, and Modjeska Simkins was elected secretary. The first president, Reverend A.W. Wright, and the first secretary, Bernice Stokes Robinson, decided to step aside because they felt Cheraw was too far from Columbia to be effective as statewide officers.

Two other activists joined the State Conference around this time. One was John H. McCray, who published a newspaper in Charleston named the *Lighthouse.* He entered into a merger agreement with attorney Earl Parker, of Sumter, who owned the *Sumter Informer,* which was managed by Osceola E. McKaine, and renamed the paper the *Lighthouse & Informer.* McCray moved the paper to Columbia and set up shop at 1022½ Washington Street. In later years, he moved the paper to 2469 Waites Road in Columbia. The other activist, Osceola E. McKaine of Sumter, had reorganized the Sumter Branch in 1940 and joined with McCray in sparking the cause of human and civil rights from the platform and press in a general way. They contributed materially to the growth and expansion of the State Conference NAACP. McCray's Waites Road address became the family home of the McBrides, who have become a dynasty in politics in Richland County, South Carolina.

The NAACP Conference has had eleven presidents. The Hinton administration, which lasted from 1941 to 1957, was marked by a period when lawsuits were the prevalent force to eliminate discrimination in the state and to truly make the Fourteenth Amendment what it was suppose to be. Between 1941 and 1957, nine major lawsuits were filed in the state during Hinton's watch. All of them were successful, as will be addressed later in this book.

Reverend I. DeQuincey Newman, the third president, from 1958 to 1960, focused on voting rights and access to public accommodations. He resigned the presidency in 1960 and accepted the executive secretary position, serving in that capacity until 1969.

The fourth president was the Reverend II.B. Sharper of Sumter. He served for a brief period during 1960. He pastored churches in Sumter and Florence and left the state in the mid-1960s.

In late 1960, J. Arthur Brown of Charleston became the fifth president of the State Conference. He was the first non-minister to head the organization. During his tenure, he addressed the issues of public accommodations and education. His administration sponsored many sit-ins, wade-ins, preach-ins and lawsuits to desegregate the Charleston public school system. His daughter was the plaintiff in one of those cases.

The sixth president, Reverend J. Herbert Nelson, a Presbyterian minister of Sumter and, later, Orangeburg, served from 1965 to 1968. His focus was voting rights. With the passage of the 1965 Voting Rights Act on his watch, he stressed getting blacks registered to vote.

The seventh president, Reverend Al Holman, an AME minister of Charleston, served from 1968 to 1969. He continued Reverend Nelson's efforts to increase voter registration rolls.

The eighth president was Reverend Matthew D. McCollom. During his tenure from 1969 to 1977, he stressed voter registration and urged blacks to run for public office. He was a United Methodist minister from Orangeburg and a great Scrabble player.

The ninth president, Dr. William F. Gibson, served for twenty years, from 1977 to 1997. He practiced dentistry in Greenville. A native of Darlington, South Carolina, he graduated from Allen University and MeHarry Dental School. He stressed economic opportunities for blacks. His activities centered on what was called the "Fair Share" program, which challenged major corporations to invest in and do business with black businesses.

The tenth president was James Gallman, an educator from Aiken. He served from 1997 until 1999. He continued the programs of Dr. Gibson.

The eleventh president, Dr. Lonnie Randolph of Columbia, came on the scene in 1999 and is currently serving as of the publication of this book. The Confederate flag was a fiery and controversial issue when he took office. It was on Randolph's watch that the flag was removed from the capitol dome and the House and Senate Chambers to the Confederate Memorial on the north side of the statehouse grounds. He continues to lead the challenge to remove it from that location and propose more sanctions against the State of South Carolina until it is removed from the statehouse grounds.

A person who did not serve as president of the State Conference was Robert Logan. Logan served as the first vice-president of the state NAACP during the 1960s and 1970s. He was from Saluda, where he operated a funeral home and other enterprises. He was a steady force and respected by all leaders in the NAACP conference. His daughter, Delores Logan, is a successful entrepreneur in Columbia.

The following is a list of executive directors/secretaries of the organization:

Modjeska Simkins, 1941–46
Eugene Montgomery, 1946–50
Al Redd, 1950–51
Modjeska Simkins, 1951–57
I. DeQuincey Newman, 1960–69
Isaac W. Williams, 1969–83
Nelson B. Rivers III, 1984–94
James L. Felder, 1994–95
Brenda Reddix-Smalls, 1995–98
Dwight James, 1998–Present

Racial tension was so extreme for the state NAACP that for many years it could not, and did not, publish its address or telephone number. For many years, the office was located at the corner of Taylor and Harden Streets, above a drugstore, with no sign to indicate it was there. However, through the years, with its successes, it moved to 2330 Main Street and, later, to 6111 Main Street, Columbia, where it is presently headquartered.

In the early days of the organization, the executive director's wife also served as his secretary. In the case of Reverend Newman, his wife, Anne, served as secretary and was the plaintiff in a major local lawsuit, *Newman v. Piggie Park Barbecue*. She won the case, and Piggie Park had to start serving blacks in its restaurants.

WITH THE ELECTION OF REVEREND Hinton as State Conference president in 1941 and Modjeska Simkins as secretary, the organization was now ready to do business and take on all comers. When Hinton moved to Columbia in 1939, he worked as the manager of the Pilgrim Health and Life Insurance Company and pastored Second Calvary Baptist Church. During his administration, chapters increased from thirteen to eighty. He was often threatened and was kidnapped in 1949 in Augusta, Georgia, but was able

Harold R. Boulware, who served as the first lawyer for the state NAACP in 1940. He became a family court judge in later years.

to escape. Shots were fired at his home in 1956 in Columbia, and today a marker at 1226 Height Street indicates where he lived during his tenure.

With the State Conference ready to make a move against discrimination in South Carolina, all it needed was a lawyer. Harold Boulware would fill that role. He grew up in Irmo, South Carolina, attended Harbison Junior College and earned a bachelor's degree from Johnson C. Smith University, the Presbyterian-sponsored college in Charlotte, North Carolina. Upon graduating from Howard University School of Law in 1939, he returned to South Carolina and became general counsel for the state NAACP. His office was located on Washington Street in Columbia. One would not think it was a lawyer's office because it was always a beehive of activity. Boulware was an army veteran, an active member of Omega Psi Phi Fraternity and an active participant in the Presbyterian Church (more about him later). He is buried in the family cemetery on the campus of Midlands Technical College, Harbison Campus, in Irmo.

2

BLACK VETERANS RETURN HOME

Upon the United States' entry into World War II, the country did not have enough soldiers in the military to fight two wars in the Pacific and the Atlantic theaters. Therefore, it was necessary to institute a draft. Black and white country and city boys alike were conscripted to serve in the U.S. Army, Marines and Navy. Black boys were sent off to Europe to fight for the rights of people over there when they did not enjoy the same rights at home. Following the war, that would change. Some questioned how the country was going to keep farm boys down on the farm when they had seen the lights of "Gay Paris." Many saw those lights and then came home to fight.

The first to come home was not a World War II veteran but a World War I veteran in the person of Osceola E. McKaine. McKaine was born in Sumter on December 18, 1892, to Selena Durant McKaine. He grew in up in north Sumter, at 714 North Main Street. He attended Lincoln High School, graduating in 1908, and left Sumter to see the world. He worked on merchant ships and in 1914 enlisted in the U.S. Army. He attended officer training school in Iowa and graduated as a second lieutenant. He was then shipped off to France, where he served as a supply officer during World War I. He took courses at Boston College and correspondence courses from other institutions of higher education. He spoke four languages and could communicate in three others.

Upon mustering out from the army in 1919, he landed in New York and immediately began organizing veterans to fight for the rights they did not have in the United States. He founded an organization called the League for Democracy. It had over three hundred members. He established chapters in many cities on the East Coast. The headquarters was located in Harlem. The purpose of the organization was for the mutual protection and advancement of the black race. It was his vision that the league would become the predominant civil rights organization in the United States. Eligibility required that one was a veteran or the family member of a veteran. McKaine also founded a newspaper in New York called the *New York Commoner*. He was active as a street corner orator, sharing his views with anyone who would listen. He became a target of J. Edgar Hoover's FBI, which did not care for his rabble-rousing, as it was called then. Dissension in the ranks of the League for Democracy caused him to shut it down and return to Europe.

McKaine settled in Ghent, Belgium, in 1924 and started up several businesses. First, he opened a nightclub called Mac's Place and later added a hotel. He would book acts from the United States when they were traveling through Europe, and he had a very successful enterprise. When the Germans invaded France in 1940, they confiscated his properties. He left Europe and returned to Sumter for the first time since he had left in 1908.

Upon landing in Sumter, he jumped right into the fight for civil rights. His first act was to reorganize the Sumter Branch of the NAACP, which had become dormant, and his cousin James T. McCain was elected president. He also found time while he was in New York in 1918 to become a charter member of Epsilon Chapter of Omega Psi Phi Fraternity. This would be the fifth chapter in the history of the fraternity, which had been founded on the campus of Howard University in 1911. He was elected keeper of records and seals.

ONE OF THE EARLY WORLD War II veterans who came home and joined Osceola on the firing line was Herbert U. Fielding of Charleston. Following D-Day in France, Fielding returned home and ran for the South Carolina House of Representatives in 1952, knowing he did not have the ghost of a chance at winning. He ran again in 1968 and lost. On his third try in 1970, he—along with James L. Felder and I.S. Leevy Johnson of Columbia—won, becoming one of the first three blacks to sit in that body since the Reconstruction era.

John H. Wrighten III of Edisto Island, South Carolina, returned home from the war and wanted to go to law school at the University of South Carolina. His application was rejected, and he sued the university and won (his lawsuit is discussed later in this book).

From Peaceful Protests to Groundbreaking Rulings

Ernest Henderson of Columbia learned to fly an airplane in 1939. He became one of the instructors of the Tuskegee Airmen at Tuskegee Institute, Alabama.

Don Frierson Sr. was a part of General George S. Patton's tank battalion in North Africa. He became so radicalized that when he returned home, he was a bitter man and shot a white soldier who called him the n-word. His son, Don Frierson Jr., hosts the *Urban Scene*, a daily radio talk show on Radio Station WGCI in Columbia. He has been on the air for over twenty years.

Lincoln C. Jenkins Jr. returned home to Columbia after the war and enrolled in Howard University School of Law. Upon graduation, he returned to his hometown, where he immediately began representing activists in the civil rights struggle. He would become a general counsel for the state NAACP.

Matthew J. Perry returned home to Columbia and enrolled in the new law school at South Carolina State College. After graduating in 1951, he opened a law office in Spartanburg, South Carolina, where he remained until 1961, when he relocated to Columbia. Perry would represent thousands of civil rights activists during the 1960s and '70s. The federal courthouse in Columbia is named the Matthew J. Perry Federal Courthouse in honor of him.

There was the Reverend D.D. Felder of Sumter, who served in the army for ten years with the Chaplain Corp. He rose to the rank of captain. When he returned home to Sumter, he jumped right into the Sumter movement, daring the police to arrest him and others who were picketing stores on Main Street. Reverend Felder was an Allen University graduate and an AME minister. After a disagreement with the presiding bishop of the AME Church, he joined the United Methodist Church, from which he later retired.

He and his wife, Lorraine, were the parents of six children. Three of the children, Leona, Daniel and Joe, became telecommunication executives. Loretta is a dentist in Columbia. Jason is a photographer, and Danielle is a social worker in Charlotte, North Carolina.

Leroy Bowman of Sumter was one of the original Tuskegee Airmen. After many years of being away, he returned to Sumter and now assists his half brother, Ralph Canty, at Jobs' Mortuary.

Charles Golden served in North Africa and the Philippines but could not find work when he returned home to Sumter. He and his wife, Lillian Felder, moved to Baltimore, Maryland, where they worked for five years, saved a small fortune and returned to Sumter, where they built a house and beauty shop with their savings. He immersed himself in the Sumter movement.

Reverend D.D. Felder was a World War II veteran and activist in the Sumter movement.

Elmore Brown returned to Charleston after storming the beaches of Normandy and joined Herbert Fielding in the Charleston movement.

Albert Kennedy of Columbia was in the first graduating class from the law school at South Carolina State College. He worked in the Richland County government and became a tax collector.

Over in Clarendon County, in the town of Summerton, Harry Briggs returned from the navy and jumped into the fight to get equal facilities for his children and others in the school system. He is the Briggs in the *Briggs v. Elliott* school desegregation case that became part of the five cases in *Brown v. Board of Education* handed down in 1954.

James Crawford of Cheraw was born in the Lowcountry of South Carolina. He learned printing at an early age and worked for newspapers in Charleston, Columbia and Indiana before settling in Cheraw, where he work at the *Cheraw Chronicle* until it was sold. He was active in the civil rights struggle, working closely with Levi G. Byrd.

J. Phillip Rembert of Sumter was a Tuskegee Airman. Upon his return to Sumter, he took a job with the post office and became very active in the Sumter movement. His involvement led to his being elected the first black to serve on the Sumter County Council.

E.C. Jones Jr., a Sumter native, returned home from the war and opened a photography studio. He would capture the civil rights movement on film as he attended NAACP meetings and conventions all over the state. He was the photographer for South Carolina State College and Claflin College. He also provided photos for the yearbooks for many of the old black high schools.

He would mentor Cecil Williams of Orangeburg. Williams, in later years, would become the official photographer for the state NAACP and a stringer for *Ebony* and *Jet* magazines, the Associated Press, the *Pittsburg Courier* and the *Afro-American* newspaper.

When Jim Sulton of Orangeburg returned home from the war, he and his brother opened a service station. He became a galvanizing force in Orangeburg and would lead a successful boycott against the white merchants who were denying black children the right to attend the better-equipped public schools (more about Sulton in the chapter on the Orangeburg movement).

Eugene Montgomery of Orangeburg returned home from the United States Marine Corp in 1946 and enrolled in Atlanta University. He returned to Orangeburg in 1948 and became the first paid executive director of the South Carolina Conference of Branches NAACP from 1948 through 1952. It was Montgomery who did most of the legwork for Dr. Kenneth Clark, in Clarendon County, who interviewed many black children using his doll test to determine how segregation affected them psychologically. Montgomery joined the U.S. Postal Service following his tenure with the NAACP. Following his postal career, he owned an insurance agency and realty company.

These are just some of the veterans who returned home and made a difference in their communities. There are many others throughout the state who played major roles in bringing about badly needed changes in South Carolina. They were determined to right the wrongs of the past. Many shed blood on foreign soils and left buddies behind. Coming home to confront racism and Jim Crowism was something they were not going to settle for.

Eugene Montgomery was field secretary for the state NAACP and did much of the ground work in the *Briggs v. Elliott* case.

3
UNEQUAL TEACHER PAY

Duval v. the Board and *Thompson v. Gibbes*

Until 1944, the salaries for black and white teachers in South Carolina were unequal. White teachers earned one-third more than black teachers and had smaller classes and better equipment in the classrooms. This all came to light one day when Modjeska Simkins was standing behind a white teacher in the teller line at a local bank and looked over the teacher's shoulder to discover that the white woman's check was almost twice the amount of her check. She knew this teacher, and she also knew that this lady had less formal education and less teaching experience than she herself had. This was in 1941. Simkins brought this matter to the attention of the state NAACP to consider for legal action.

Black teachers in South Carolina during those years were members of the Palmetto State Teachers Association (PSTA), their trade organization. The name would change in later years to the Palmetto Education Association (PEA). The group's leadership was conservative and was not a proponent of rocking the boat. It had no interest in initiating any kind of lawsuit against white authorities.

In the spring of 1941, a group of younger teachers in the PSTA independently approached Osceola McKaine and asked him to help them prepare a salary equalization lawsuit. James T. McCain, Osceola's cousin, known to his friends as "Nooker," was teaching at Morris College in Sumter and was a leader of this faction. McKaine agreed to take on this task, and he began traveling the state gathering the data that would be needed to document the inequities in black teachers' pay. When he returned from Europe, he had brought with him a small fortune, and he absorbed his own travel expenses as he canvassed the state.

McKaine was involved in raising the funds to underwrite the cost of the equalization campaign. He sought the help of S.J. McDonald Sr., a leader of the Sumter NAACP and chair of the state NAACP executive committee, to assist in the fundraising efforts. McDonald contacted a group of black Sumter professionals and businessmen. Ten of these men promised to provide sufficient funds to cover any outstanding and unexpected costs that might arise. This anonymous group came to be called the "Ten Angels," and each made initial donations of $100. Some of those donors were S.J. McDonald Sr., Dr. S.J. McDonald Jr., attorney E.A. Parker, Dr. B.T. Williams, Dr. Edmond McDonald Sr., Edmond P. Palmer, Dr. E.C. Jones Sr., James T. McCain and Osceola McKaine.

One of the above benefactors, E.A. Parker, made another contribution to the civil rights cause in late 1941. Parker was a leading black attorney in Sumter and South Carolina for a long time. To supplement his law practice, he served as a pastor and presiding elder in the AME church. He also published a weekly newspaper, the *Sumter People's Informer*. McKaine hoped that Parker would work as the local attorney for the teacher equalization suit, as well as publicize the cause in his newspaper. Parker declined to serve in a formal legal capacity because of advancing age. Also, the *People's Informer* was

John H. McCray, publisher of the *Lighthouse & Informer.*

in poor fiscal shape, and he was seeking a merger with another newspaper, the *Charleston Lighthouse*, published by John H. McCray. Parker took McKaine with him to Charleston for a meeting with McCray in McCray's office at 54 Line Street. The two publishers agreed to a merger, and the *Lighthouse & Informer* was born. They decided that the combined paper would be the official organ for the teachers' equalization drive. McKaine joined the staff as head of the Sumter Bureau. It was at this time that McCray and McKaine commenced a close professional relationship that would last a lifetime. McCray moved the *Lighthouse & Informer* to Columbia, where it was easier to cover the state.

In June 1942, McKaine was invited to Columbia for a two-day meeting with the State Conference NAACP executive committee and Thurgood Marshall. S.J. McDonald asked for a motion to publicly endorse the "equal pay project" that McKaine had been promoting for a year. The motion was passed. Marshall outlined what needed to be done at the local level. The two most important acts were raising a defense fund and finding a plaintiff who could withstand the reprisals, rebukes and scare tactics that would confront him or her. Once these matters were in place, Marshall would make legal counsel available from the NAACP staff.

By late summer 1942, McKaine had completed all the necessary field research for the lawsuit. He continued traveling the state, reaching out to black organizations such as the Congaree Medical, Dental and Pharmaceutical Society and the Baptist Educational & Missionary Convention. These groups not only endorsed "the cause" but also made financial contributions to the Teachers Defense Fund. The list of donors was keep confidential so as to protect contributors from retaliation by irate white authorities. Funds were raised at public rallies and mass meetings by passing the hat. With funds raised, research data in hand and the endorsement of the NAACP, the next step was to find a plaintiff. McKaine wanted someone from Sumter to play that role but could not find a taker. At the quarterly meeting of the state NAACP held in Sumter in February 1943, the committee decided to take over the search from the Sumter Branch and expand it into other parts of the state. Conference president James M. Hinton thanked the Sumter Branch for its dedicated work and announced that a female plaintiff had been indentified in Charleston.

During the course of this equalization pay effort, three plaintiffs were involved in three different proceedings. They were Melissa T. Smith and Viola Duval of Charleston and Albert N. Thompson Sr. of Columbia.

The first plaintiff, Melissa T. Smith, was a graduate of South Carolina State College and had taught at Burke High School for four years. She was brought to the South Carolina Conference NAACP annual meeting in Florence in 1943 by Jesse E. Beard, president of the Charleston Branch. She met privately with Thurgood Marshall and Harold Boulware. It was planned that she would take a one-year leave of absence and attend graduate school at Columbia University in New York City. She would leave for New York five days after her salary equity petition was filed with the Charleston School Board. NAACP officials thought it desirable that Smith be out of South Carolina while the suit was progressing so that she would not be subjected to professional and social ostracism by her frightened colleagues and public harassment by white racists angered by the litigation. On June 24, 1943, Smith's petition for salary equity was delivered by registered mail to Dr. A. Burnett Rhett, superintendent for the City of Charleston Schools. This document was prepared by Boulware for "Melissa T. Smith individually, and on behalf of the Negro public school teachers and principals of the City of Charleston Schools." The petition stated that "the School Board and Superintendent had for many years maintained a policy of paying Negro teachers and principals of Charleston less salary than white teachers with equal qualifications and experience and performing the same duties." Boulware added bluntly that this difference in pay was "based solely on race and color." He further wrote that this policy clearly violated the equal protection clause of the Fourteenth Amendment of the U.S. Constitution. In conclusion, the petition demanded "that immediate action on this petition be taken at the School Board's next meeting in order that the petitioner's legal rights in the premises may not be jeopardized by further delay."

On August 6, 1943, at a special meeting, the Charleston County School Board did an end run around Smith's petition. In order to avoid dealing with the racial aspects of salary inequities, it adopted a resolution eliminating race or color references on applications for employment. All teachers and principals of the district would be graded and classified in respect to their certificates, preparation, teaching abilities and general fitness. This was a subjective approach to the matter, and it would give the school board another way to pay black and white teachers different salaries. This tactic had been used by other southern states to avoid equal pay for black and white teachers. While the lawyers were jockeying for position, Melissa Smith decided she did not want any part of this anymore. In September, she informed President James M. Hinton, of the state NAACP, that she was taking a full-time teaching position in New York City. The time had come to start a new search for a plaintiff to start the matter all over again.

Again with the help of Jesse E. Beard, president of the Charleston NAACP, a new plaintiff was located by the second week of October 1943. Thurgood Marshall and Harold Boulware traveled to Charleston to interview Viola Louise Duval. Ms. Duval was a graduate of Howard University and had taught chemistry at Burke High School for three years. The legal team was pleased with the interview with Duval, and preparation began for another try at equal pay for teachers and principals. When the Charleston School Board denied Duval's petition, a lawsuit was filed in the Federal District Court for the Eastern District of South Carolina. Both sides agreed that the litigation would be resolved by a consent decree and would not be appealed by the losing party. The official title of the lawsuit was *Duval v. Seigneus*, and it was scheduled to be on the court docket for February 1944.

During the period leading up to her court date, Duval discovered that she had become persona non grata to many of her black teaching associates in Charleston County. She was shunned by her fellow teaching associates and neighbors, who were fearful of the stand she was taking. She was especially shaken when one of her female colleagues who shared yard patrol duty with her at Burke High School stopped speaking to her. While she was an active member of the Palmetto State Teachers Association, the organization made no gesture of support on her behalf. A rumor was circulating in Charleston that any black educator found supporting the Duval cause would be promptly fired. Various white supremacists sent hate mail to her, and she was forced to live in seclusion.

On the day of the trial, February 10, 1944, John H. McCray and Osceola McKaine, of the *Lighthouse & Informer*; Modjeska Simkins; and Thurgood Marshall and his legal team traveled to Charleston together. This was Marshall's first trial in South Carolina, and he did not know what to expect. He and his team immediately learned that the judge for the case was J. Waites Waring, a federal judge appointed by President Franklin D. Roosevelt in 1942. The local community did not think he was a liberal judge but did not know what to expect from him on the bench. They were encouraged when they learned that the first act by the judge was to desegregate the courtroom. Also, he had appointed a black bailiff.

Waring was a Charleston aristocrat who had spent all of his years practicing law in Charleston. He had served as the corporation counsel for the city. For the first fifteen minutes of the hearing, according to John McCray, Waring left Harold Boulware, Edward Dudley and Cassandra Marshall shocked and Thurgood Marshall surprised beyond all words. Waring began the trial by facing the lawyers representing the school board. He asked them to recall the date of the Alston decision, which had been sustained by the U.S. Supreme Court. The Alston decision was a case in Norfolk, Virginia, in which the plaintiff sought equal teacher pay and was granted the same. When Marshall stood to answer, Judge Waring said to him curtly, "I did not ask you, Mr. Marshall." After fumbling through some documents, the defense lawyers found the answer and told Judge Waring that the date was 1940. Waring then asked the defense counsel when the Montgomery County, Maryland teacher equalization pay lawsuit was decided. Again, Marshall attempted to answer the question, and Judge Waring ordered him to be silent. After that, Marshall and his staff sat confused and bewildered, according to McCray. At this point, the black observers in the courtroom were muttering to one another. One woman sitting next to Modjeska Simkins shouted out, "See there, child! They don't even let her lawyer talk. Dear Jesus!"

McCray recalled that he was clearly disturbed by Judge Waring's conduct. Duval was sitting behind her attorneys and was about to cry, frustrated by all that was taking place in front of her. In contrast to the black observers, the white observers were smiling with pleasure. Eventually, the defense lawyers told Judge Waring that the Maryland case had been handed down on July 30, 1937. At that point, Waring swung his chair around to Marshall and his team and said:

> *Mr. Marshall, I don't want you to think I was being rude in not permitting you to answer those questions. I knew you knew the answers. I was trying to determine how long it has been that the school board of Charleston has known that it must pay equal salaries to all of its teachers. This is a simple case, and there is no need to take up the court's time. I have a question for you. What kind of order do you want entered? Do you want salaries equalized immediately? Do you want to give the board some time to equalize?*

A stunned Marshall, standing with his mouth open, finally said that he needed to confer with his legal team before giving an answer. Waring told Marshall he wanted a written answer in his office in three days and announced abruptly that court was adjourned. Judge Waring had awarded black South Carolinians their first major legal victory in civil rights in over five decades. It only took him fifteen minutes to do it. McCray reported that pandemonium broke out in the courtroom. Suddenly, Duval was surrounded by well-wishers. He further reported that a woman was heard to say, loud enough to be heard across the Cooper River, "Child, I was with you all the time, but I could not show my hand!"

Judge J. Waties Waring was the federal district court judge who ruled in favor of blacks in the five cases that came before him between 1944 and 1951. He had to leave the state because of his rulings.

The white political power structure of South Carolina was outraged by Waring's decision. However, within a year of the salary equity ruling, Waring divorced his wife of thirty-two years and married a twice-divorced northern Yankee, Elizabeth Avery. It was that act that commenced his bitter break with most of his longtime friends in Charleston.

Viola Duval did not remain in South Carolina following the lawsuit to enjoy the fruits of her labor. She met her future husband, Nathaniel C. Stewart Sr., on a blind date while he was serving with the Tuskegee Airmen at a military base in Walterboro, South Carolina, fifty miles north of Charleston. They were married on August 14, 1945, and later moved to Philadelphia, his hometown, so that he could attend pharmacy school. He graduated and went on to become the first African American department head at Philadelphia General Hospital as the director of pharmacy services. Now Viola Duval Stewart, she took a teaching position in the public schools and retired in 1981. In 1938, at Howard University, Mrs. Stewart was initiated into the Alpha Chapter of the Alpha Kappa Alpha Sorority, and she remained active throughout her life. Her last "night out" was spent celebrating her seventieth year in the sorority at its centennial gala in Washington, D.C. She died on December 14, 2010. She is buried in Chelten Hills Cemetery near Germantown, Maryland.

The third plaintiff in these equal pay lawsuits was Albert N. Thompson of Columbia. This action, *Thompson v. Gibbes et al*, was necessary because the

Duval case only affected black teachers in Charleston County. This case was heard in Columbia, and Judge Waring presided. Thompson was a graduate of Tuskegee Institute in the class of 1940. After graduation, he returned to Columbia and taught at the Booker T. Washington Heights Elementary School. His wife was a graduate of Benedict College, and she taught in Richland School District 1 as well. In Thompson's suit, Judge Waring simply cited the Duval case and ruled in his favor. After his successful victory, Thompson was fired from Richland District 1 and had to seek employment in small rural schools outside Columbia. Once those districts found out that he was the plaintiff in that lawsuit, he was dismissed. He had taught in Edgefield and Chester Counties. Everywhere he went, the lawsuit followed him. In 1948, he left South Carolina and journeyed to New York, where he enrolled in New York University and earned an MS, followed by an MS from Boston College and finally a PhD from the University of Pittsburgh. He moved his family to Houston, Texas, where he would complete a fifty-year teaching career at Texas Southern University, retiring in 1999. He returned to South Carolina often, and when he died in 2004 at age eighty-four, the family brought his remains back to Columbia for burial in historic Randolph Cemetery. He was a member of Omega Psi Phi Fraternity. His son, Albert N. Thompson Jr., is chair of the Chemistry Department at Spellman College in Atlanta. He was most helpful in providing information that helped account for his father's tenure in Columbia.

Harold Boulware, chief counsel for the state NAACP, did not participate in the Thompson case. Following the Duval case, Boulware was drafted into the army. However, he would return for the next series of lawsuits in Judge Waring's court.

4

THE LAW SCHOOL AT
SOUTH CAROLINA STATE COLLEGE

Wrighten v. USC Board of Trustees

Before the dust settled on the teachers' equal pay cases, John H. Wrighten III was knocking on the doors of the University of South Carolina School of Law seeking admission. Wrighten was a native of Edisto Island, South Carolina. He was the eighth of nine children. The family had a small farm, and he and his siblings worked the farm while his father worked as a day laborer. In those days, that was a reasonable and comfortable existence. As a result, Wrighten was able to attend Avery Institute in Charleston. Following service in World War II, he completed his senior year at Avery and made plans to attend college. Upon graduation, he sought admission to the all-white College of Charleston, Judge Waring's alma mater. While in high school, he had been a member of the Charleston NAACP Youth Council, and it made him become kind of a militant fellow. The College of Charleston delayed giving him a decision, so he enrolled at South Carolina State College in Orangeburg. After a year at South Carolina State, he and two friends applied to the College of Charleston again and were denied. By this time, the black leadership in Charleston put pressure on him and the others to cease their efforts in gaining admission. They were told that all of their activities were jeopardizing Avery Institute and race relations in Charleston.

Wrighten returned to South Carolina State College, and prior to his graduation in 1946, he sought admission to the University of South Carolina Law School, the all-white and only law school in South Carolina. His application was promptly denied on the grounds of his race. He then contacted Harold Boulware, the NAACP legal counsel who had returned from military service, and asked him to file a lawsuit on his behalf against the university.

As early as 1938, the U.S. Supreme Court had handed down a decision in the case of *Gaines v. Canada*, which held that states must furnish separate but equal law schools for both races or admit blacks to their all-white institutions. In its lawsuit, the NAACP lawyers demand that the university admit Wrighten or create a law school for him and his race. In addition to Boulware acting as Wrighten's counsel, there was W.F. Robinson of Columbia, Earl A. Parker of Sumter and Thurgood Marshall and Robert Carter of the New York NAACP office. Again, Judge Waring would step into the picture. By now, the Old Charleston aristocrat had become persona non grata in the white community of Charleston—and statewide, for that matter. They turned on him after his divorce, and the invitations to parties and other social events stopped coming. Waring resigned from the Charleston Club, the South Carolina Society and the St. Celia Society of Charleston. He literally had no white friends in Charleston anymore. So, he struck back and began to have dinner parties at his home at 63 Meeting Street for black friends. Some of his close black friends were Septima P. Clark and J. Arthur Brown, who would later become president of the Charleston Branch and State Conference NAACP. Others included his bailiff, John Fleming; Ruby Cornwell, wife of Dr. A.W. Cornwell, a local dentist; and several others. For Waring's courage, he would be honored by black newspapers around the country, including the *Chicago Defender*, *Color* magazine and the *Afro-American* newspaper. Omega Psi Phi Fraternity honored him and his wife at a mass meeting at Morris Street Baptist Church and bestowed on him the organization's Citizen of the Year Award.

Waring scheduled a hearing for the case for June 19, 1947. In anticipation that something like this would happen in the courts, in 1946 the General Assembly had appropriated $60,000 for the creation of a graduate and law school at South Carolina State College. At a pre-trial hearing, the parties agreed that the plaintiff would challenge only the adequacy of the facilities for the potential law students and not the constitutionality of segregation itself. After Waring issued an order confirming the pre-trial agreement, Robert Carter wrote to Waring indicating that his team wanted to challenge the "sufficiency and quality" of any school that would be built or used. The judge responded that he was going with the pre-trial agreement that had been made, and that was that.

At the hearing, the state said it had planned to establish a black law school at Orangeburg, but to date no blacks had sought a legal education there.

The first class of law students at the new law school at South Carolina State College. Seated in the center is the dean, Dr. B.C. Turner.

Wrighten's lawyers stated that their client desired immediate admission to the University of South Carolina Law School since there was not a black law school in operation. On July 12, 1947, Waring rejected Wrighten's lawyers' request and said that, in view of the circumstances, it was only fair to give the state until September 1947 to open the Orangeburg law school. He issued an order that had three options: number one, they admit Wrighten to the University of South Carolina; number two, they build him a law school at South Carolina State College; or number three, if they didn't do either, he would close the University Law School. That was on July 14, 1947. In September 1947, two months later, South Carolina State College opened its law school with a dean and three faculty members. There was no building and no library, and John H. Wrighten III refused to attend.

In 1948, the General Assembly appropriated $200,000 for a building and $30,000 for library acquisitions. Up to this time, the law school was operating in a corner of the administration building, Wilkinson Hall. By the fall of 1949, a two-story building had been constructed on the campus. Wrighten enrolled that year and graduated in 1952. After failing the state bar exam the third time, Wrighten wrote to the dean of the University of South Carolina Law School. He said that given his poor performance on the bar exam, South Carolina obviously had provided him with an inferior education at South Carolina State Law School. He said he would be soon seeking admission to the University of South Carolina Law School or its Journalism School. In a few months, he was allowed to take the bar exam a fourth time, and on that occasion he passed.

Wrighten practiced law in Charleston and Walterboro. He was active in voter registration drives. In 1957, he and several other black Charleston lawyers registered over two thousand persons of color in Charleston County. In 1959, he opened a law practice with Russell Brown. Upon Wrighten's death, Brown said, "When it comes to black lawyers he was considered to be the granddad of us all." He represented civil rights protestors and other civil rights matters. When he retired from the practice of law, he pastored AME churches in New London, Connecticut. On October 3, 1996, he died in Sumter, South Carolina, where he was living with one of his sons.

The little law school at South Carolina State College that Thurgood Marshall called a $1.50 law school lasted from 1947 until 1966. During that time, fifty men and one woman earned law degrees there. It produced distinguished graduates who would turn South Carolina upside down legally. They included U.S. District Court judge Matthew J. Perry; South Carolina Supreme Court chief justice Ernest A. Finney Jr.; South Carolina Circuit Court judge Daniel E. Martin Sr.; Family Court judge Ruben L. Gray; Family Court judge Willie T. Smith and Court of Appeals judge Jasper M. Cureton, who attended the law school for one year and, knowing that it would close, sought admission at the University of South Carolina Law School.

Cureton earned a bachelor's degree in agriculture from South Carolina State. He applied to the USC Law School and was denied admission. But he was persistent. He had Matthew Perry write the dean a letter of reference. The dean met with Cureton and asked what his scores were on the LSAT. His scores were already on file since Cureton had a copy sent to USC. Dean Robert McFig pulled his application and said, "Damn, your scores are higher than any of my students here at USC." Cureton was admitted and graduated, becoming the first black person to graduate from the USC Law School since Reconstruction.

Many of the law school graduates left the state and migrated to other states. Paul Webber III became a superior court judge in Washington, D.C. Colonel Ned Felder served as a military judge in the U.S. Army. Talmedge Bartell served as a military lawyer. Bassey Mbrey was a lawyer in Nigeria. Allen A. Christian practiced law in the Virgin Islands. George Anderson practiced law and ran the Community Action Agency in Aiken, South Carolina. Weldon Hammond served as an adjudicator for the U.S. Veterans

Administration Regional Office in Columbia for over thirty years. Zack Townsend set up shop in Orangeburg and represented many of the sit-in protestors in that city. Franklin DeWitt returned to Conway and practiced law there until his death. The one female graduate of the law school was Laura Ponds of Camden, South Carolina. The last report on her was that she was employed by the U.S. Department of Housing and Urban Development in Philadelphia.

5

THE RIGHT TO VOTE

Elmore v. Rice

Following the Civil War, Congress passed three amendments to the U.S. Constitution. The first was the Thirteenth Amendment, which freed all slaves, male and female. The second was the Fourteenth Amendment, which granted equal protection under all the laws of the federal and state governments. The third was the Fifteenth Amendment, which guaranteed the right to vote to black males only. (Women, both black and white, did not gain the right to vote until 1920 with the passage of the Nineteenth Amendment.) With the passage of these three amendments, black men not only began to vote but also ran for and were elected to public office. During a ten-year period from 1867 to 1877, which some called the Reconstruction era and W.E.B. Dubois called the mystic years, men of color held office in the state legislature, the U.S. Congress and county and local offices. Jonathan J. Wright sat on the South Carolina Supreme Court, and Richard T. Greener taught metaphysics at the University of South Carolina. Francis L. Cardoza served as secretary of state and later as state treasurer. Alonzo J. Ransier was lieutenant governor and later served one term in the U.S. House of Representatives. During this period, more black men from South Carolina than from any other southern state served in the U.S. Congress.

The demise of black political participation began when the incumbent governor, Republican Daniel Chamberlain, was challenged by Democrat Wade Hampton III. The Hampton forces used every violent means available to intimidate and discourage blacks from voting. Stuffed ballot boxes in Edgefield County provided Hampton with a margin of victory. In some counties, there was a larger number of votes cast than there were registered voters. The election was close, and both sides claimed victory. For a short period of time, South Carolina had two governors.

In the presidential election of 1876, a race between Democrat Samuel Tilden of New York and Republican Rutherford B. Hayes of Ohio was close because of the voting irregularities in the South. The election was thrown into the U.S. House of Representatives. The southern members agreed to support Hayes if this would end Reconstruction. The Compromise of 1876 was struck. The Democrats supported Hayes in exchange for removing the federal troops from the South. By 1896, blacks had lost all the gains acquired during Reconstruction and would be subjected to a new kind of slavery called Jim Crowism and the black codes. George Washington Murray of Sumter, a distant cousin of Jim Clyburn, would be the last black to serve in the U.S. Congress in 1897.

The passage of the South Carolina Constitution of 1895 was the final nail in the coffin to discourage black political participation. It set the following requirements for all voters: a minimum age of twenty-one years, a state residency of two years, a county residency of one year and a poll tax paid six months prior to the general election. If a person of color could meet all of these requirements, then there was the problem of the literacy test. This test required blacks to demonstrate proficiency in both reading and writing by copying a section of the state constitution chosen by the election registrar. And if one were able to meet all of the above requirements, there was still this matter of being excluded from voting in the state Democratic Party primary. The existence of the white state Democratic Party primary was to ensure that blacks were disenfranchised because this barred blacks from participating in the only election that had any actual significance. For the next fifty years, blacks in South Carolina would not be able to participate in the voting and political process of South Carolina.

Fast-forward to 1944. That was the year when John H. McCray and Osceola McKaine of the *Lighthouse & Informer* newspaper decided to organize a black political party, which they named the Progressive Democratic Party. This was an idea that A.J. Clement of Charleston had proposed in 1942. After organizing the party, they elected delegates and sent them to the 1944 Democratic National Convention in Chicago. At that convention, they challenged the regular democratic delegates from South Carolina. The challenge was not successful, but they received national attention, and new focus was placed on South Carolina and its dirty politics. Twenty years later, Fannie Lou Hamer of Mississippi would repeat this action at the Democratic National Convention in Atlantic City when she and her Mississippi Freedom

Democratic Party delegates challenged the Mississippi Regular Democratic Party delegates.

Also in 1944, Osceola McKaine ran against Olin D. Johnston for a seat in the U.S. Senate. He did not win, but his effort increased black voter registration all over the state. His run was a precursor to Jesse Jackson's run for president forty years later in 1984, when black voter registration skyrocketed. While McKaine's effort was not successful, it planted a seed that encouraged others to challenge the all-white Democratic Party primary. George Elmore of Columbia got the message. He attempted to vote in the 1946 Democratic Party primary and was denied. He had the NAACP file a lawsuit on his behalf in the U.S. District Court of South Carolina Eastern Division. This case would become the landmark case of *Elmore v. Rice*. His legal team was Harold Boulware of Columbia and Thurgood Marshall and Robert Carter of the NAACP New York office. And the judge in the case was none other than Judge J. Waties Waring. This case and the Wrighten one were on the docket to be heard by federal judge George Bell Timmerman Sr. Timmerman was a member of the USC Board of Trustees, so he excused himself from the Wrighten case and asked Judge Waring to hear it in his place. Waring saw the Elmore case on the docket and asked to hear that case, as well. Timmerman agreed.

Elmore v. Rice was not a difficult case for Waring, although it was an interesting one. Thurgood Marshall and his legal eagles had already dismantled the all-white Democratic Party primary in Texas in the case of *Smith v. Alwright* and in Georgia in the case of *King v. Chatman*. Judge Waring listened to the arguments of both sides and then uttered the following: "It has been stated and I believe it is a fact that South Carolina is the only state which now conducts a primary election solely for whites. Since the 'classic' case, Negroes are voting in Louisiana primaries. I cannot see where the skies will fall if South Carolina is put in the same class with these other states." He closed his comments by saying, "It is time for South Carolina to rejoin the Union. It is time to fall in step with the other states and adopt the American way of conducting elections." He granted George Elmore and others similarly situated in Richland County the right to participate in the Democratic Party primary elections.

It was necessary to file a second lawsuit, *Brown v. Baskin*, since the Elmore decision only covered Richland County. In the second case, Waring again listened to both sides. About this time, it appears that Waring had reached the limit of his tolerance on this voting stuff. He closed the hearing with the following:

It is the intent of this opinion that the full spirit hereof, as well as the mere letter, be obeyed so that the democratic organization of South Carolina and the primaries which it holds shall be freely open to all parties entitled to enter therein under the laws and constitution of this country and this state, without discrimination of race, color or creed. Any violation of the terms of the order or the law set forth in this opinion, by them or their successors in office, or those acting under them, will be considered a contempt and will be proceeded against and punished.

The action by the white power structure in South Carolina was swift and furious. Congressman L. Mendel Rivers of Charleston demanded that Waring resign from the bench. When Waring refused, Rivers started a fund to raise money for impeachment proceedings against the judge. South Carolina newspapers assailed him. The KKK stepped up its intimidation acts, burning crosses in front of his house. The U.S. Marshal Service had to assign special police to guard the Waring house on Meeting Street in Charleston. His circle of friends got smaller and smaller, and the invitations to social functions stopped coming. But Judge Waring was not yet finished, for over in Clarendon County, *Briggs v. Elliott* was beginning to simmer.

The tragic part of most of these cases was that the plaintiff who won the lawsuit suffered economic and social reprisals afterward. George Elmore did not escape this fate. Elmore was born on March 31, 1905, in Holly Hill, South Carolina, and grew up in Harleyville, South Carolina. In 1922, he moved to Columbia, where he met and married Laura Belle Delaney. He was a very successful businessman in Columbia. He owned two liquor stores and a five-and-dime store and controlled two Blue Ribbon cabs and a photographic studio. However, after he filed the lawsuit, distributors stopped delivering products to his stores. Banks cut off his credit. His house was foreclosed on. His wife suffered a mental breakdown and spent the rest of her life in institutions. The children were sent to live with relatives. On February 25, 1959, he died while living in his truck. Many in the black community were shamed by his fate, but no one lifted a finger to help him in his time of need. Elmore is buried in historic Randolph Cemetery in Columbia. In recent years, a monument was erected at his grave site to remind the public of his civil rights efforts. In June 2007, the South Carolina Voter Education Project honored George Elmore by awarding him the organization's Trailblazer Award posthumously.

Osceola McKaine, who was a friend and mentor to George Elmore, did not enjoy the victory of Elmore's 1947 case. He had departed for Europe in the fall of 1946 to see what he had left of his businesses there after World War II. Upon his arrival, he found that his partner had been able to salvage some of the business. The economy was bad, so he began to sell off some of his assets. First, he sold the hotel named the Artisan's Inn. He then reduced the number of employees at Mac's Place, his restaurant. He began to transfer portions of his personal savings to Victory Savings Bank in Columbia, South Carolina, which was controlled by his friend and former employer's relative Modjeska Simkins. Finally, he and his partner decided to file for bankruptcy. He began to make plans to return to South Carolina in the summer of 1955. In November 1955, he collapsed on the street in Brussels. He was rushed to the hospital, where he died several hours later. The U.S. State Department notified his half brother, Ferdinand Abraham, who lived in Sumter and worked as a professor of music at Morris College. Abraham arranged for Palmer Memorial Funeral Home to handle the funeral. The eulogy was delivered by John H. McCray, McKaine's longtime friend. Ferdinand Abraham played an organ rendition of the old spiritual "Going Home." McKaine was buried with full military honors in Walker Cemetery in the Abraham family plot. He was sixty-two years old when he died.

6

UNEQUAL EDUCATION

Briggs v. Elliott

I t was June 1947 when the Reverend J.A. DeLaine, an AME preacher, and some dirt farmers in Clarendon County lobbed the first grenade at the wall of public school segregation in South Carolina. DeLaine, who was also a public school teacher, was attending a summer school session at Allen University in Columbia when an assembly was called to hear the Reverend J.M. Hinton, president of the South Carolina Conference NAACP, present a message on the problem of segregation in the public schools of South Carolina. Hinton stated that the NAACP was looking for persons to be plaintiffs and petitioners in lawsuits to challenge the status quo. He urged those in attendance to return to their communities and find individuals to participate in this cause.

The Reverend DeLaine accepted the challenge and returned to Summerton in Clarendon County, where he organized a committee to meet with the superintendent of schools. The committee's initial request was a simple one: since there were no buses to transport black children to school, some of whom had to walk nine miles a day one way, it asked for a bus. The white students had thirty-seven buses that would drive by the walking black children and splash them with mud when it rained on the old dirt roads. The superintendent and school board said no. An appeal to the State Department of Education in Columbia brought the response that it was a local matter and out of its hands. An appeal to the U.S. Justice Department in Washington brought the same response. Some of the farmers in the Jordan and Davis Station area of the county pooled their money and bought an old school bus. It broke down a lot. The committee went back to the superintendent and

Justice Thurgood Marshall was the national NAACP counsel and participated in all of the legal cases in South Carolina from 1944 to 1954. In this photo, he is addressing a mass meeting at Claflin College in Orangeburg. President Lyndon Johnson appointed Marshall to the United States Supreme Court in 1965. *Courtesy of Cecil Williams.*

reported that it had purchased a bus and asked if he would provide gasoline. Superintendent L.B. McCord, a Presbyterian minister and administrator of the county schools, said no again.

Reverend DeLaine and several of the farmers journeyed to Columbia for a meeting with Harold Boulware, the NAACP lawyer, seeking a resolution to this matter. Boulware wrote several letters to the school board, and when he received no responses, he filed a petition on March 16, 1948, in the U.S. District Court in Florence, South Carolina, in the name of *Levi Pearson v. Clarendon County Board of Education*. When the news broke in the *State* newspaper, Levi Pearson became a hero among his people. The celebration lasted for three months. On June 8, 1948, the petition was thrown out of court on a technicality. Pearson's property spread over School District 5, where he paid taxes. His children attended school in School District 26. Therefore, he was held to have no legal standing to bring this case. Reprisals started immediately.

When planting time came that spring, Pearson found that his credit had been cut off by every bank and merchant in the county. He had enough money put aside for seeds for the cotton, tobacco, oat and wheat planting, but he did not have enough for fertilizer. He had to cut down some of his timber and sell it to raise some cash. When the pickup man came from the mill—the same mill that belonged to R.W. Elliott, who would later become the defendant in *Briggs v. Elliott*—he learned why Pearson was selling it, and he drove away, leaving the timber lying in the field. That autumn, Pearson could not find a white farmer who would let him use a harvester to bring in his crops as he had always done in the past. He had borrowed money from his neighbors in the spring to buy fertilizer and now he had to watch his crops rot in the fields. Finally, the white merchants in the county told Pearson that if he would just forget about the buses and the NAACP and tend to his own business, everything would be taken care of again. This would be the end of round one.

Round two began the following spring. This time, the stakes were higher, and the whites were watching. Almost a year following the Pearson disaster, in March 1949, Reverend DeLaine and a few of the farmers were invited to a meeting in Columbia with top state and national officials of the NAACP. This meeting featured Thurgood Marshall, whose successes as a civil rights lawyer had turned him into a legend. A little bit disappointed by the setback in the bus case the previous year, Marshall was too seasoned a battler to be discouraged for very long. To tie a test case to a single plaintiff was always risky business. It was too easy to find some disqualifying ground, as had been done with Levi Pearson, or to intimidate the plaintiff into dropping out. This time, they would seek a firm, unified group of twenty plaintiffs or more.

And this time, they would not settle for a few battered buses. The schools in Clarendon County were a plain disgrace. Anyone could see it, and now the black community was going to ask for equal treatment from top to bottom: new buses, new buildings, equal teacher pay, classroom materials and so on. Anything less would be in violation of the Fourteenth Amendment. Marshall explained to the group that if they could assemble at least twenty sturdy plaintiffs who would stay the course, the NAACP would bring a major test case here in South Carolina; if not, he would take the fight elsewhere. During a break, the Clarendon delegation huddled. They decided that they would accept Marshall's challenge and headed back to Summerton.

For the next eight months, Reverend DeLaine and Reverend J.W. Seals, also an AME minister at St. Mark AME Church, traveled the length and breadth of the county seeking signers for the petition. The two preachers reminded one of the cartoon characters Mutt and Jeff. Reverend DeLaine was tall and erect, and Reverend Seals was short and stocky. People were reluctant to sign the petition. They remembered what had happened to Levi

Pearson. However, on November 11, 1949, DeLaine had more than the twenty names Thurgood Marshall needed to go to court.

Legal custom dictates that in a lawsuit with multiple plaintiffs, the case is cited after the first name on the complaint. Heading the list in alphabetical order was Harry Briggs, then a thirty-four-year-old navy veteran with five children. He had always lived in Summerton, except for the time he spent in the South Pacific with the navy. For fourteen years, he worked at the Carrigan Service Station in Summerton on Main Street, across from the Piggly Wiggly food store. He pumped gas, repaired tires and greased cars. After signing the petition, his boss called him in one day and told him he did not need his services anymore. He said he wanted a boy to work for him. He could not afford Briggs any more. It was Christmas Eve, and his boss gave him a carton of cigarettes and said goodbye.

Harry's wife, Eliza, had worked for six years at the motel down on Highway 15 in Summerton. The motel owner told her there was a lot of pressure being put on him to have her take her name off the petition. She told him that she did not sign the petition. He said, "But your husband did." She countered that her husband was old enough to have a mind of his own, and she was not going to tell him to take his name off. Her boss gave her a week's notice, and she was gone. As fate would have it, Harry Briggs's cow

This photo features the Reverend J.A. DeLaine, leader of the Clarendon County effort to desegregate schools, and Harry and Eliza Briggs, plaintiffs in the *Briggs v. Elliott* lawsuit. *Courtesy of Cecil Williams.*

got loose and stepped on a gravestone in the McClary family cemetery plot. The town's lone policeman came and arrested the cow. The whites thought that was funny as hell. Harry Briggs had to sweat plenty before he got his precious cow back.

The reprisals did not stop. Up in Manning at the Fleming & DeLaine Funeral Home operated by Billie Fleming, a cousin of Reverend J.A. DeLaine, Fleming learned that black sharecroppers on some farms were no longer allowed to bring their dead to his funeral parlor. One family brought in a dead infant for burial after the lawsuit was filed but had to switch the body to another funeral home when the white boss who was going to pay the bill found out. The reprisals continued. Reverend DeLaine was hit with a $20,000 libel suit by the black principal at Scotts Branch High School. It was reported that the principal was pocketing student fees, and when this came to light, he blamed DeLaine for releasing the information. Reverend DeLaine, his wife and two sisters were fired from their teaching positions in the county.

Things got so tough for DeLaine in Summerton that his supervisor, Bishop Frank Madison Reid Sr. of the AME Church, transferred him to St. James AME Church in Lake City, thirty-five miles northeast of Summerton. It was one of the churches his father had founded.

On November 17, 1950, Judge Waring told Thurgood Marshall to change his complaint. Instead of simply asking for equal facilities, he should challenge the constitutionality of segregation in the public schools of South Carolina. Marshall was a bit reluctant to do such a thing for fear that they would lose at every level. He did not want a second defeat in Clarendon County in a two-year period. Over dinner at Judge Waring's house in Charleston, Marshall agreed to make the changes.

When the constitutionality of a state law or statute is challenged in the federal courts, it requires a three-judge panel to hear the matter. Since this complaint fell into that category, three judges were appointed to hear the case. They were Judges John Parker, chief judge of the U.S. Fourth Circuit Court of Appeals, and George Bell Timmerman Sr. and J. Waties Waring of the U.S. District Court of South Carolina. Parker had been denied a seat on the U.S. Supreme Court following challenges of his racist views by the NAACP. Timmerman was known as an avowed segregationist from Batesburg, South Carolina. A hearing date was set for May 28, 1951, in Charleston. The morning of the hearing, a caravan of little old cars traveled from Summerton to Charleston. In a courtroom that seated only seventy-five people, some five hundred stood in the hallways and outside on the streets. The court did not hand down its decision until June 21, 1951. In a two-to-one decision, Parker and Timmerman upheld segregation. Judge Waring wrote a dissent abolishing segregation of the races in the schools of South Carolina. He filed a twenty-one-page dissenting opinion, his last and most important decision as a judge in South Carolina. Part of the dissent reads as follows:

> *There is absolutely no reasonable explanation for racial prejudice. It is all caused by unreasoning emotional reactions and these are gained in early childhood. Let the little child's mind be poisoned by prejudice of this kind and it is practically impossible to ever remove these impressions, however many years he may have of teaching by philosophers, religious leaders or patriotic citizens. If segregation is wrong then the place to stop it is in the first grade and not in the graduate colleges. From their testimony, it was clearly apparent, as it should be to any thoughtful person, irrespective of having such expert testimony, that segregation in education can never produce equality and that it is an evil that must be eradicated. This case presents the matter clearly for adjudication and I am of the opinion that all of the legal guideposts, expert testimony, common sense and reason point unerringly to the conclusion that the system of segregation in education adopted and practiced in the State of South Carolina must go and must go now. Segregation is per se inequality.*

Judge Waring moved out of South Carolina after writing those words. As fate would have it, his dissent or minority opinion in this case would become the unanimous opinion when it reached the U.S. Supreme Court and was joined by the other four cases that became *Brown v. Board of Education.* He moved to New York and continued to hear cases in the federal courts there for the next sixteen years. Federal judges are appointed for life. Since Congressman L. Mendel Rivers could not get him impeached, Waring continued to serve as a federal judge until his death. Upon his death in 1968, his body was returned to Charleston for burial in Magnolia Cemetery, north of Charleston on Meeting Street. Fewer than a dozen whites attended the graveside service. However, on hand were more than two hundred blacks who had formed a motorcade at St. Mathews Baptist Church following a memorial service for Waring that was orchestrated by J. Arthur Brown, president of the Charleston NAACP, and I. DeQuincy Newman, executive director of the state NAACP. All came to say farewell to a judge who had refused to be corrupted by his own white society.

Four months following the hearing in Charleston, Reverend DeLaine's home in Summerton went up in flames. Members of the all-white Summerton Fire Department were on hand as the wood-frame house burned to the ground. They made no effort to put out the fire because DeLaine's house, they said, was beyond the town's limit. It was one hundred feet outside the city limits. At this time, DeLaine was still preaching in Lake City. Once the locals there found out who he was, harassment began. Shots were fired into his house. His church in Lake City was burned. One evening, a car drove slowly past his house and fired several shots into the house. DeLaine fired back, hitting two of the assailants. The lone black policeman on the Lake City Police force came by and warned DeLaine that maybe he should leave town. DeLaine got into his Ford Mercury and drove to the home of William Bennett in Florence, the only black lawyer in town at that time. Bennett escorted him to Charlotte, North Carolina, where some relatives whisked him away to Washington, D.C., and finally to New York. He would never return to his native state. An arrest warrant was issued, but Governor Nelson Rockefeller refused to grant extradition, and DeLaine remained out of reach of the South Carolina authorities until his death. While in New York, he and Judge Waring got together often. DeLaine founded an AME church in Buffalo, New York. It is named DeLaine-Waring AME Church.

Reverend J.A. DeLaine died on August 3, 1974, in Charlotte, North Carolina, and his funeral was at Greater Bethel AME Church. No denominational dignitaries eulogized him, and there was scarce notice of his demise. However, since his death, roads and monuments have been erected in his name in South Carolina, some say a little bit late.

Another family that played a part in the Briggs case was that of Henry F. Brown and Thelma McDowell Brown. They were the parents of twelve children. Six of the children and their parents signed the petition for the Briggs case. Henry Brown would pay a price for his family's actions. He was the custodian for the white Summerton High School. In addition to his cleaning and maintenance of the building, he also played the piano for school programs and school dances. In his early years, he was a traveling musician and played for the legendary Bessie Smith. When he would not remove his name from the petition, he was fired by the school district. It might have been a blessing in disguise in one way. Now he was able to devote full attention to his farm, blacksmith shop and sugar cane mill.

The Brown children were Henry E., Geneva, Nathaniel, Eva, Howard, Beatrice, Harrison, Marian, Ethel, Maxine, Vera (who died during her senior year of high school) and Thomas. Nine of the twelve children attended college. The Browns are a close-knit family, and they return to Summerton every Mother's Day and Thanksgiving. Beatrice, the seventh in the family chain, relocated to Summerton after forty years in Washington, D.C., working for the federal government in the CIA and Labor, Commerce and EEOC Departments. She lives on the old family estate and is president of the Summerton Rotary Club.

THERE HAVE BEEN SOME POSITIVE changes in Clarendon County since the Briggs case. At the school superintendent level, Broadus Butler, Al Swinton, Elijah McCants, Rose Wilder and John Tindal, all blacks, have served in the school districts of the county. Rose Wilder was the first black person to serve as president of the Summerton Rotary Club. Manning's first black mayor, Kevin Johnson, was elected to the South Carolina House of Representatives in 2011, another first. He was replaced in the mayor's office by a black female, Julia Nelson. In the county courthouse, Hayes Samuel is the coroner, Pat Pringle is the auditor, Beaulah Roberts is clerk of court and Leon Richburg is the veterans service officer.

Not all of the whites in Clarendon County were evil and mean-spirited. The Land family, who operated an oil jobber business, did sell fuel to blacks during the struggle in the 1940s. Many blacks did not forget the Lands' good gesture. They showed their thanks by electing and reelecting John C. Land III to the South Carolina Senate for forty years. Clarendon is one of the black-majority counties in the state.

7

DESEGREGATING THE BUS

Flemming v. SCE&G

S arah Mae Flemming, a native of Eastover, South Carolina, is one of the forgotten heroines of the civil rights movement. She was an outspoken pioneer who is not in the history books. Flemming's story was revealed when Lauren Markoe, a reporter for the *State* newspaper, discovered some stories about her and compiled an extensive article that ran in the paper on March 30, 2003.

Ms. Flemming, a black domestic worker, took a seat in the front of a Columbia bus operated by the South Carolina Electric & Gas (SCE&G) Company on June 22, 1954. This was a full year and a half before Rosa Parks boldly made her famous stance in Montgomery, Alabama. On that June morning, the bus was crowded, and blacks were standing in the aisle. When a seat became vacant near the front, Ms. Flemming sat down. She testified in her trial that the driver immediately said to her, "Get up and move to the back, and I mean now." When she got up to exit out the front door because the back was crowded, the driver confronted her and punched her in the stomach. He then made her leave by way of the rear door. She went to see a doctor to determine if any ribs were broken. When the doctor released her, she went to the room she rented during the week. (She would go home to Eastover on weekends.) She placed an ice pack on her stomach to ease the pain for the rest of the evening.

In those days, the State of South Carolina had a law that allowed bus drivers to, in effect, serve as police officers on the bus. Their word was final, and if one refused to comply with their demands, he could be convicted of a misdemeanor.

Modjeska Simkins was in her thirteenth year as secretary of the state NAACP when she heard of the situation with Sarah Flemming and the run-in she had with the bus driver. Mrs. Simkins called a young white lawyer in Columbia and asked him to represent Flemming in a civil case against the bus company. She knew Philip Wittenburg because he had represented another black women who had been fined for sitting in the front of a bus. This lady was convicted, but on appeal, the prosecutor, in order to avoid fighting a challenge to segregation, dismissed the case on a technicality. Wittenburg talked to Flemming and agreed to take her case. Simkins paid the legal fees.

On July 24, 1954, the lawyer filed suit in the U.S. District Court for South Carolina in Columbia, asserting that Sarah Mae Flemming's civil rights had been violated under the Fourteenth Amendment to the U.S. Constitution and its equal protection clause. He also asked for $25,000 in damages. The case was scheduled for a hearing before Judge George Bell Timmerman Sr., the same judge who had ruled against the plaintiffs in *Briggs v. Elliott* in 1951. Judge Waring had left South Carolina by now and was hearing cases in New York. Judge Timmerman was living in the Governor's Mansion with his son, George Bell Timmerman Jr., who was elected governor following Governor Jimmy Byrnes. Timmerman dismissed the case, stating that the *Brown v. Board* case was about education, and this case was about transportation.

Wittenburg had no federal appeals court experience. Mrs. Simkins called her friends in New York at the NAACP national office, Thurgood Marshall and Robert Carter, and asked them to join in the appeal. Wittenburg traveled to New York City to meet with Marshall, Carter and Spottswood Robinson. All three of these men would become federal district court judges. The team prepared a brief for the U.S. Court of Appeals, and Wittenburg was ready to argue his case. Since Wittenburg had not practiced before the U.S. Fourth Circuit Court of Appeals, which sits in Richmond, Virginia, he needed someone who was approved by the court to offer a motion to allow him to argue his case before the court. Even though the lawyers from SCE&G were from Columbia and knew Wittenburg, they refused to offer the motion for him to argue the case. Robert Carter, NAACP lawyer, moved that Wittenburg be allowed to argue the case before the court. The U.S. Court of Appeals heard the case and overruled Timmerman's dismissal, sending it back to him for a trial on the matter.

On the evening of June 12, 1956, Wittenburg was watching television at home with his wife and infant daughter. Suddenly, he heard commotion outside and looked out the window. There stood an eight-foot cross burning on his front lawn. Some of his neighbors gathered to watch. The telephone rang, and the caller identified himself as a member of the KKK. He threatened to kill Wittenburg and his family if he didn't drop the case. The next day, the young lawyer went to court. Everyone had heard about what happened to him the night before, but no one spoke a word about it in Judge Timmerman's court.

On June 13, 1956, the case was set for trial a second time, and Timmerman dismissed the case again. It was at this point that the pressure on Wittenburg was too much. He decided to drop the case.

Enter Matthew Perry and Lincoln C. Jenkins Jr., young black attorneys eager to advance civil rights through the courts. Jenkins, a native Columbian, World War II veteran and graduate of Howard University School of Law, returned home to practice law. Matthew J. Perry, a native Columbian, World War II veteran and graduate of South Carolina State College Law School in 1951, had set up a practice in Spartanburg, South Carolina. This case would bring these two lawyers together, and shortly thereafter they would form the law firm of Jenkins & Perry in Columbia. Later, Hemphill Pride II would join that firm, and they would handle most of the civil rights lawsuits of the 1960s.

Jenkins and Perry picked up where Wittenburg left off. They appealed Timmerman's second dismissal to the U.S. Court of Appeals in Richmond. Again, the appellate court ruled in Flemming's favor and ordered Timmerman to hold a trial on the merits of her case. The appellate court ruled on the constitutional question presented in Flemming's favor, but the issue of damages had to be tried back in Timmerman's court. Matthew Perry said, "Timmerman found us very objectionable. He ruled against us at every turn." An all-white male jury found SCE&G not guilty, and Sarah Mae Flemming never saw the $25,000 she sought in the lawsuit. Timmerman, an ardent segregationist, stayed on the court until 1963, when he retired. However, before he retired, he orchestrated the ouster of the minister of his church because the clergyman was opposed to segregation. Timmerman died in 1966.

On the basis of the Flemming case, whereby the appellate court upheld her right to sit where she pleased on the bus, the U.S. Supreme Court ruled against the Montgomery, Alabama bus company that denied Rosa Parks her seat on its buses.

Sarah Mae Flemming quickly faded from the public conscious and seemed to push the incident to the back of her mind. She was known throughout the Eastover community as a warm, loving person but also as a person who was not afraid to speak her mind. After the case was over, she said, "I will never ride a city bus again." She died on June 13, 1993, and is buried in Goodwill Baptist Church on Highway 76/378, just before crossing the Wateree River heading to Sumter.

As for SCE&G, in 1966 it hired its first black bus driver, Johnny Pough. Some other early drivers included Johnny Kinlock, James Smith, Ernest Dessasure and Willie McMillian. In administration, there were Dave Coleman, Charles and Darlene Gary, Kenny and Mamie Price, Melvin Washington and Homer Mitchell.

In 1984, SCE&G AND ITS subsidiaries became wholly owned by SCANA Corp., now a Fortune 500 company employing over 5,800 people. SCANA made news in 2002 when the company informed its employees that they could not display Confederate flags on their cars in company parking lots. SCANA also forbid employees from parking company cars in the lots of Maurice Bessinger's restaurants on their lunch breaks, but they could park off-site and eat there.

Bessinger flew Confederate flags at his restaurants and distributed literature claiming that slavery was God's will and that black people were happy to be slaves. In 1966, Ann Newman, the wife of Reverend I.D. Newman, NAACP executive director, sued Maurice Bessinger's Piggie Park restaurants in a case known as *Newman v. Piggie Park* and won the right to be served inside the restaurants. Prior to that, blacks could only purchase barbecue for takeout. In October 2002, SCANA turned over the operation of the bus system to the Central Midlands Regional Transportation Authority.

On September 23, 2005, the South Carolina Voter Education Project honored Sarah Mae Flemming posthumously with its Trailblazer Award for the contribution she made toward equal justice for people of color in South Carolina. Also at that event, Philip Wittenburg, the young white lawyer who first represented Ms. Flemming, was given the organization's Legacy Award. Wittenburg move from Columbia to Sumter, where he practiced law for many years. He now lives on Hilton Head Island.

8

NAACP MEMBERS PUNISHED

In 1956, two years after the U.S. Supreme Court handed down *Brown v. Board* outlawing segregation in public schools, the State of South Carolina was still angry at the court and the NAACP. It could not do any harm to the court, so the powers that be took out their anger on the NAACP and its members. The General Assembly passed a law on April 19, 1956, prohibiting any government employee—city, county or state—from holding membership in the NAACP.

The first casualties of this law were twenty-one teachers at Elloree Training High School in Elloree, South Carolina, near the eastern edge of Orangeburg County. Prior to the end of the school year and summer vacation, employee contracts for the next year were passed out, along with a questionnaire, to all the teachers. Those who planned to return in September were requested to complete these documents and return them to the superintendent. The questionnaire asked the following:

1) Do you favor integration of the races in South Carolina?
2) Do you feel you would be happy in an integrated school system knowing that parents and students did not favor this system?
3) Do you feel that you are qualified to teach an integrated class in a satisfactory manner?
4) Do you believe in the aim of the NAACP?
5) If you join the NAACP while in this school district, would you notify the superintendent and trustee board?

The teachers who were fired from their jobs for being members of the NAACP in Elloree, South Carolina. *Courtesy of Cecil Williams.*

There were thirty-one teachers at the school, and twenty-one of them refused to sign the documents for the next school year. Some of the protesting teachers said they were not members of the NAACP, but they refused on grounds of principle. Dr. Walker E. Solomon, executive director of the Palmetto Education Association (PEA), met with the school principal and teachers, NAACP members, Lincoln C. Jenkins Jr. (NAACP chief counsel) and Thurgood Marshall. Jenkins and Marshall filed a lawsuit in the U.S. District Court challenging the school contract and the entire process. While the lawsuit was working its way through the courts, the PEA assisted the teachers in finding jobs in other counties and out of state. The principal, Charlie Davis, was hired by the American Friends Service Committee. When the South Carolina General Assembly met in 1957, the law was repealed.

The next one to get the axe for not renouncing her NAACP affiliation was Septima P. Clark of Charleston. Mrs. Clark had an early, long history with the NAACP. She was one of the early members of the Charleston Branch when it was organized in 1917. Initially, she taught on John's Island and later worked at Avery Institute in Charleston. It was during this time that she secured the signatures of over twenty thousand persons to present to the

Dr. Walker E. Solomon Sr. was executive director of the Palmetto Education Association (PEA), the black teachers' organization.

school board, petitioning it to hire black teachers in the Charleston County school district. At that time, only white teachers taught in black schools. She moved to Columbia in 1927 and was very helpful in organizing support for the teachers' equal pay lawsuit. In 1956, she was fired from her teaching position because she would not renounce her NAACP affiliation. She was not deterred. She went to Tennessee and worked at the Highlander Folk School training civil rights advocates on how to assist their communities in registering blacks to vote. One of her star pupils was Rosa Parks. In 1962, she wrote her autobiography, *Echo in My Soul*. She taught on Defauski Island for a period of time and then joined Dr. Martin L. King in the Southern Christian Leadership Conference (SCLC), where she taught in citizenship schools in Georgia and South Carolina. At age seventy-six in 1974, she was elected to the Charleston County School Board. She was also a member of the delegation that accompanied Dr. King to Oslo, Norway, when he received the Nobel Peace Prize in 1964.

Septima P. Clark was fired from her teaching position for failing to renounce her membership in the NAACP. She joined Dr. Martin L. King's SCLC organization and continued her battle to educate blacks on the need to register and vote.

After much prodding from black members of the South Carolina General Assembly, in 1976 she was awarded the one-year salary in the amount of $3,000 that she would have earned had she not been fired from her teaching position. She served on the board of directors of the Penn Center at Frogmore on St. Helena Island in Beaufort, South Carolina. Even though she did not drive a car, she never missed a board meeting and would take the Greyhound bus, with her grandson David in tow, when she could not get a ride to take her the sixty miles from Charleston to Beaufort.

The College of Charleston bestowed an honorary doctorate upon her in 1978. It was the first time a person of color had been so honored by that institution. Mrs. Clark died on December 15, 1987, and is buried in Old Bethel United Methodist Church Cemetery in Charleston. She was a member of the Alpha Kappa Alpha sorority.

OVER IN SUMTER, JAMES T. McCain, cousin of Osceola McKaine, was elected president of the Sumter NAACP Branch in 1938. He worked as dean at Morris College in Sumter until 1949, when he left to become principal of Palmetto High School in Mullins, South Carolina. When the school board learned about his NAACP affiliation, he was asked to write and sign a statement saying he had nothing to do with the NAACP lawsuit *Brown v. Board*. He refused. The school board fired him. He then became principal of Scotts Branch High School in Summerton, where the *Briggs v. Elliott* lawsuit originated. Again, he was dismissed because of his NAACP connections. McCain then join Alice Spearman at the South Carolina Council on Human Relations, an organization recently founded to improve race relations in the state. He remained in that position for two years.

In 1957, James Farmer, president of CORE (Congress on Racial Equality), hired McCain as a field director for the southern states. McCain traveled the South training people for nonviolent direct-action protests. He was the mastermind behind the Freedom Rides. When the freedom riders arrived in Rock Hill, South Carolina, in 1961, McCain dragged future South Carolina Supreme Court chief justice Ernest A. Finney Jr. out of a social function in Sumter to go to Rock Hill to meet the riders.

McCain conducted a workshop in Mississippi the week before Chaney, Goodman and Scherner, the three young men who died in Mississippi during the freedom summer (1964), met their fate.

When CORE had its split in 1969, Roy Ennis took the action arm of CORE, and Ronnie Moore took the education arm, and they went in separate directions. McCain convinced Jim Felder to spend six months with the Scholarship, Education and Defense Fund for Racial Equality

James T. McCain was fired from several teaching positions in South Carolina because of his NAACP affiliation. He served as southern field coordinator for the Congress On Racial Equality (CORE) for twenty years.

(SEDFRE), the education division, directing a project to identify Hispanic school board members across the United States. The project ended with a conference of Hispanic school board members in Washington, D.C., in 1969, a first of its kind for Hispanics.

James T. McCain passed away on June 5, 2003, at age ninety-eight. He is buried in Hillside Memorial Park in Sumter.

ANOTHER DEFIANT PERSON WHO REFUSED to renounce her NAACP membership was Gloria Rackley Blackwell. Blackwell was a native of the Little Rock section of Dillon County. She graduated from Lincoln High School in Sumter and Claflin College in Orangeburg. She later earned a master's degree from South Carolina State College and a doctorate from Emory University in Atlanta. In 1963, she was declared unfit to teach and fired from her teaching position because she was a field organizer for the NAACP.

Her activism started in the early 1960s, when she was arrested for sitting in the whites-only waiting room of the Orangeburg Regional Hospital. She had taken her daughter Jamal to the emergency room for an injured finger.

Gloria Rackley Blackwell and her daughter, Lurma, walking beside the school from which she was fired because of her NAACP activities. *Courtesy of Cecil Williams.*

Her attorney, Matthew J. Perry, defended her so vigorously and argued her case so forcefully that he was cited for contempt of court. The case was dropped shortly thereafter, and she filed a civil lawsuit and won the case against the hospital.

After being fired by the school board, Blackwell worked for the NAACP as a field organizer, traveling all over the state in a small Chevy, sometimes with students from Claflin or South Carolina State College, urging parents to fight for the rights of their children to be enrolled in the white public schools. Her daughters, Lurma and Jamal, became regular protesters on the picket lines—so much so that Lurma was sentenced to reform school for having a lengthy arrest record at age thirteen.

On December 7, 2010, Gloria Rackley Blackwell died from heart failure at Piedmont Fayette Hospital in Atlanta. She donated her body to Emory University and the Morehouse College School of Medicine for research purposes. Blackwell was honored in Dillon, South Carolina, on January 15, 2011, with a parade and memorial service. Her daughters and Jim Felder spoke at the services.

9

THE SIT-INS

There are some events in life that capture your attention, and you remember them forever. The John F. Kennedy and Martin Luther King assassinations are two examples. You remember exactly where you were and what you were doing on those days. For Jim Felder, February 1, 1960, is added to that list. On that date, four young men in Greensboro, North Carolina, all freshman at A&T State University, decided to stage a sit-in at the Woolworth's Department Store in downtown Greensboro. It touched off what would become the sit-in movement that raced like wildfire across the South. These four students were Joe McNeil, Ezell Blair, Frank McCain and David Richmond. They had no plan and no preparation but just decided that they would sit at the lunch counter in Woolworth's that day.

Felder was a twenty-year-old student in his junior year at Clark College in Atlanta, and this particular day he was in Washington, D.C., attending his first Supreme Council meeting with the other officers of the Omega Psi Phi fraternity at its national headquarters. The previous December (1959), he had been elected as second vice grand basileus at the organization's national convention in New York City. This post gave him a seat on the board representing undergraduate fraternity members all over the country.

The Supreme Council was in its first session when suddenly Ellis F. Corbett, the editor of the *Oracle*, the fraternity's magazine, was pulled out of the meeting to take a telephone call from the president of A&T State University. Corbett's daytime job was as public relations officer at the school, and the president summoned him back to Greensboro to deal with the press and media on the sit-ins. There were several other college presidents at that meeting, and they thought it wise to return to their campuses. The meeting broke up.

Felder returned to Atlanta, where he served as president of the Student Government Association at Clark College. He found Julian Bond and Lonnie King of Morehouse College waiting for him. They huddled at Yates & Milton Drugstore, a hangout for students, across the street from both campuses, and began the initial planning for the sit-ins for the students in the Atlanta University Center. Later, Marian Wright Edelman, a Bennetsville, South Carolina native and Spelman College student; Don Clark of Morehouse; Mary Ann Smith of Morris Brown College; Willie Mayes of Atlanta University; Roslyn Pope of Spelman; and Marion Bennett of the Interdenominational Center would join in the planning.

There were six Historical Black Colleges and Universities (HBCUs) in Atlanta at that time: Atlanta University, Clark College, Morehouse College, Morris Brown College, Spelman College and the Interdenominational Center (ITC). The first decision made by the group was that all the schools should be involved in what was called the Atlanta movement. Meetings were held with the student leaders from all campuses. Plans were made for the assault on downtown Atlanta stores. The college presidents got wind of the plans and asked for a meeting with the leaders of the student bodies.

A meeting was held with the six presidents of the Atlanta University Center. At that meeting were Clement of Atlanta University, Brawley of Clark, Mays of Morehouse, Middleton of Morris Brown, Manly of Spelman and Richardson of ITC. Initially, they tried to discourage the students from going ahead with the sit-ins in Atlanta. One must remember that these were bricks-and-mortar men, and the survival of their institutions depended on not just tuition but also grants and contributions from corporations and foundations. They did not want to poison the stream from which they were drinking at the time.

After lengthy discussions, and when they realized that the students' minds were made up to move forward, Dr. Benjamin E. Mays rose and stated that if they were going to do it, they needed to outline their goals and objectives before going out on the streets so they could respond intelligently when a reporter stuck a microphone in their faces. The student leaders drafted an outline of their concerns and had it published in the *Atlanta Journal & Constitution* at a cost of $1,200. It was titled: "An Appeal for Human Rights." It was signed by the student government presidents of the six Atlanta University Center schools. The next day, the *Wall Street Journal* and *New York Times* ran the article full page at no cost. With that done, the Atlanta student movement was off and running.

From Peaceful Protests to Groundbreaking Rulings

In other communities and on other college campuses, students did not always consult with administrations or faculty but just took off marching to the downtown area. There were many names for protests. In Nashville, it was the Nashville movement. In Orangeburg, it was the "Orangeburg 7" coordinating the activities. In Rock Hill, it was the "Friendship Nine"—and so it went.

The sit-ins caught fire and spread throughout the South. In the words of Victor Hugo, "There is nothing more powerful than an idea whose time has come." It was truly a student-inspired movement, and these students had nothing to lose, no property, no fear of job reprisals and the fearlessness of youth. They took on the establishment and won.

There were some efforts by the old-line organizations—CORE, SCLC and NAACP—to co-op the students and make the sit-ins a part or division of their respective programs. Ella Baker, who came to Atlanta to assist Dr. King set up the administrative side of SCLC, advised the students to form their own organization. Baker was a seasoned veteran of civil rights. She had done fieldwork for the NAACP in the 1940s, organizing branches throughout the South. She was a graduate of Shaw University in Raleigh, North Carolina, and when she sought permission from her alma mater to host a meeting of student leaders from around the South, it was granted. On the weekend of April 15–17, 1960, hundreds of students attended that meeting, and the Student Nonviolent Coordinating Committee (SNCC) was born.

Marion Barry, a student at Fisk University in Nashville, Tennessee, was elected the first chairman. Later, in the fall of 1960, a meeting was held in Atlanta on the campuses of Clark College and Morehouse College. It was at that meeting that Marion Barry, a chemistry major headed for graduate school, stepped down as chairman of the SNCC. Later in life, Barry would be elected to the Washington, D.C. school board and city council and serve twenty years as mayor of the nation's capital. He suffered some brushes with the law, but the citizens of D.C. returned him to city council after his term as mayor; he continues to serve on the council as of this writing.

Chuck McDew, a student at South Carolina State College in Orangeburg, followed Barry as chairman and served from 1960 to 1963. He was replaced by John Lewis in 1963; Lewis served until 1966. During Lewis's tenure, he had the pleasure of attending the March On Washington on August 28, 1963, where Dr. King gave his "I Have a Dream" speech. Lewis also participated in the first Freedom Rides. He was beaten to a pulp—and stutters today because of it—on the March from Selma to Montgomery, Alabama, for voting rights. After serving the SNCC, Lewis was elected to the Atlanta City

Council, and in 1986, he was elected to the U.S. Congress from Georgia, where he still serves.

In 1966, Stokely Carmichael replaced Lewis as chairman and took the organization in a more militant direction, away from its course of nonviolent direct action. It was Stokely who coined the phrase "Black Power." It was at this time that the SNCC began to move toward its grave and ultimately demise after H. Rap Brown took over the reins. The SNCC died a quiet death, and many of its leaders began to take part in the political process.

Julian Bond, an early organizer of the SNNC, served in the Georgia legislature for more than twenty years after fighting in the courts to take his seat because he refused to be drafted into the U.S. Army. He served for many years as board chair of the national NAACP. Today, he is a professor at the University of Virginia.

Lonnie C. King Jr., who chaired the Atlanta students' "Appeal for Human Rights" committee, served as president of the Atlanta Branch NAACP for many years and challenged the Atlanta School Board on many of its policies. Today, he is retired in Atlanta.

Ben Brown of Atlanta was another early leader in the SNCC and the Atlanta movement. A graduate of Clark College and Howard University School of Law, he was one of the masterminds who helped Jimmy Carter get elected president in 1976. Brown served in the Georgia legislature for over fifteen years and was appointed vice chairman of the Democratic National Committee by President Carter. He also served as an advisor to the president. It was through Ben Brown's efforts that President Carter was convinced to appoint twenty-two black federal judges on the same day in 1977, more than all of the presidents combined from George Washington to Gerald Ford.

A South Carolinian who played a major role in the SNCC was Cleveland Sellers of Denmark, South Carolina, who served as communications director for several years. Today, he is president of Voorhees College in his hometown. As a fifteen-year-old high school student in Denmark, he led demonstrations in that city.

The SNCC was never a structured organization with a 501(c)(3) tax-exempt status. It was a movement for a specific purpose, and when that goal was accomplished, it faded away as most movements do. There was never any constitution or bylaws, no hierarchy at the top that issued orders to the bottom. All voices were equal in the SNCC, and it moved its protest activities to where the need was greatest. The SNCC produced many of the future leaders of this country. A few have been named here, but there were many others in various communities who will be discussed in the chapters on movements.

10
THE CHARLESTON MOVEMENT

B lack Charlestonians, who are a proud lot, will not hesitate to share their history with you. They are quick to point to Denmark Vesey, who planned a movement to free the slaves in Charleston in 1822. His plan was to immobilize Charleston security forces and load all the slaves on ships and take them to Haiti. Vesey bought his freedom after winning $1,500 in the 1800 East Bay Street lottery. He spoke several languages, was a great orator and was a member of the African Church, which later became the African Methodist Episcopal Church (AME). His plot failed when a house slave informed his master of the plans, and the Charleston Police quickly rounded up the leaders of the movement. Vesey was hanged, along with twenty-two of his collaborators.

Black Charlestonians will remind you that the first AME Church in South Carolina was founded by Morris Brown in Charleston. Brown would later become a bishop in the AME Church but was exiled from South Carolina following Denmark Vesey's plot because the establishment thought he was part of it.

They will quickly point to Richard Cain, another AME pastor, who came to South Carolina following the Civil War and resurrected the AME Church, which had been banned in the state for forty years following Vesey's plot. Cain hired Vesey's son Robert to build Emanuel AME Church, which is located on Calhoun Street in downtown Charleston. Cain also founded the town of Lincolnville in the northern part of Charleston County. It was the first all-black town in South Carolina with its own elected officials.

The first NAACP branch in the state was established in Charleston in 1914 by Edwin Harrelston, who became its first president. Harrelston was an artist and mortician. The name of J. Arthur Brown is a revered one in Charleston. Brown was president of the Charleston NAACP for many years during the 1940s and '50s and was the first layperson elected State Conference president in 1965. Brown led many protests to dismantle segregation at lunch counters, state parks and golf courses and in the public school system. His children were plaintiffs in two of the school cases.

Leaders of the 1940s and '50s in Charleston included A.J. Clement of the North Carolina Mutual Life Insurance Company; "Big" John Chishom, president of PAC; Septima P. Clark; Bernice Robinson; Dr. Frank Veal; Dr. B.J. Glover; Esau Jenkins; Albert Brooks; and Herbert U. Fielding. The sit-ins brought in new younger, impatient leaders who were ready to march, demonstrate and go to jail. When the jails filled up because the courts would not accept any more property bonds, Herbert Fielding took a charter flight to Columbia for a meeting with Willis Johnson, owner of Johnson Funeral Home. In a two-hour period, Johnson worked the telephones, calling other black business and professional men, and raised $100,000. He placed the money in a suitcase and sent Fielding back to Charleston to post bail for the demonstrators, among whom was Reverend I.D. Newman.

Youth and young adult leaders would rise to the top in the 1960s. One such leader was Isaac W. Williams of North Charleston, whose involvement in the NAACP Youth Council and College Chapter would lead him to becoming the executive director of the state NAACP. Another young leader was Nelson B. Rivers III of Bennetts Point, South Carolina, who after reorganizing the North Charleston NAACP Branch, followed Ike Williams as executive director of the state NAACP. Rivers was later elevated to Southeast regional director and worked from the Atlanta office. Later, when he was promoted to the number-two position of the national office of the NAACP, he moved to Baltimore.

Young adult leaders were the forces behind the 1199 Hospital Strike in 1969. Mary Moultrie, Bill Saunders and Jim Clyburn were the leaders at the local level. The 1199 strike came about when twelve black hospital workers were fired by state government from the Medical University of South Carolina (MUSC) for union organizing and petitioning the administration for a raise to $1.25 per hour. Joining their cause was Coretta Scott King, widow of Dr. Martin L. King, who had been assassinated one year earlier. Joining her were Andy Young and Reverend Ralph D. Abernathy, president of the Southern Christian Leadership Conference (SCLC). When the hospital refused to negotiate, marches and demonstrations began in the city. Reverend Abernathy addressed a crowd of over 2,500 strike sympathizers at Morris Brown Baptist Church. In response to this, five thousand heavily armed National Guard troops were ordered into the city by the governor, and a night curfew was enforced. The protest continued. On April 30, 1969, Coretta King led a group of demonstrators, estimated at 1,500, toward the hospital from Emanuel AME Church, which is known as the "Mother of AME Churches" in South Carolina. The demonstrators were met again by national guardsmen with fixed bayonets and an armed personnel carrier to turn aside what the local newspaper described as "black rebels." Mrs. King was not arrested, but Reverend Abernathy and 900 others were jailed. The wage dispute was eventually settled when HEW secretary Robert Finch stepped in and resolved it to the satisfaction of the workers and MUSC.

Accompanying Coretta King and Reverend Abernathy to Charleston was a young fellow from Louisiana named Robert Ford. Following the strike, Ford decided to make Charleston home. He was hired by the United Methodist Church to work as a community developer. He became very involved in Charleston's political and civic activities. Later, he was elected to the Charleston City Council, and in 1992 he won a seat in the South Carolina Senate, where he has continuously served. Some recognize Ford as a civil rights battler, and others see him as a political ruffian. While he is

Coretta Scott King, widow of Dr. Martin L. King, leading a march in Charleston for the hospital strikers of the 1199 Union in 1969. *Courtesy of Cecil Williams.*

committed to the civil rights efforts, his methods are questioned by some and praised by others.

One of the leaders of the 1199 Strike, Bill Saunders, would be elected to the South Carolina Public Service Commission and become a partner in Radio Station WPAL in Charleston. Jim Clyburn, also a leader of the strike, would be elected to the U.S. Congress (more on Clyburn in a later chapter).

Other leaders who emerged from the 1199 Strike included George Payton, a South Carolina State College Law School graduate who ran against Congressman L. Mendel Rivers in 1968 and for the South Carolina Senate in 1974. He lost both of those races. In 1975, while sitting in his law office, he was assassinated, and the crime has never been solved. Isaiah Bennett, a labor organizer, ran for a seat on the Charleston County Council without success. However, Marjorie Amos would win a seat on the county council in 1974.

Lonnie Hamilton, a teacher of music in the public schools of Charleston, won a seat on the Charleston County Council in an at-large election in 1970. A renowned musician, he plays a lot of jazz in the Charleston area.

At the judicial level, Richard E. Fields, who turned ninety-one years of age on October 2, 2011, became the first black municipal court judge in South

National guardsmen block students from marching in the Charleston Hospital Strike in 1969. *Courtesy of Cecil Williams.*

Carolina in 1967. Judge Fields, a graduate of Howard University School of Law, went on to become the first black family court judge for Charleston County, and the South Carolina General Assembly elected him to the state circuit court several years later. Arthur McFarland followed Richard Fields on the municipal court bench and served as chief judge of that court for many years.

Bernard Fielding, of the Fielding Home for Funerals clan, was elected county probate judge and served for two terms.

Danny Martin Sr., after serving a stint in the South Carolina House of Representatives, was elected to the South Carolina Circuit Court and served until he retired. His son, Danny Martin Jr., now sits on the South Carolina Family Court.

After Herbert U. Fielding helped open the door for blacks to the South Carolina legislature in 1970, twelve other persons of color have taken seats in the General Assembly from Charleston County at different times. Fielding and McKinley Washington served in the House and then the state senate. Robert Ford served in the senate only. In the House of Representatives were Robert Woods, Tobias Gadson, Danny Martin, Floyd Breeland, David Mack, Lucille Whipper, Seth Whipper, Robert Brown, Curtiss Inabinett and Wendell Gillard. Timothy Scott served one term in the South Carolina House as a Republican, the first since Reconstruction.

In law enforcement, Charleston appointed its first black police chief, Rueben Greenberg, in 1982.

11

THE COLUMBIA MOVEMENT

U nlike Charleston, blacks in Columbia were not known for staging a lot of protests. In many ways, they felt insulated from the prejudices of the white community because of the economic and educational institutions in their own neighborhoods. There were powerful black economic engines in the community. If one needed banking, there was Victory Savings Bank, the only black commercial bank in South Carolina. Founded in 1921, it survived the Great Depression and the "banking holidays." If one needed insurance and home mortgages, there were North Carolina Mutual Life Insurance and Pilgrim Health & Life Insurance. If there was a need for furniture and dry goods, there was Leevy's Department Store on Assembly Street. Higher educational institutions included Allen University and Benedict College. For healthcare, there was the full-service Good Samaritan Hospital. Unemployment was always low in Columbia because of the many government agencies. There were city, county, state and federal jobs. And there was the largest training military post in the country, Fort Jackson, nearby. If one desired to dine out, there was A&B House, Chef, Pig Trail Inn, Fountainbleu Inn and the Town & Tourist Restaurant. Blue Ribbon Taxi Company provided rides for those who did not have cars. The Prince Hall Masonic Temple was the place for large meetings.

When the sit-ins erupted in 1960, they awakened black Columbia to the fact that, with all they possessed, they were still being denied equal protection and equal opportunity under the law. Yes, they had won the Elmore case, but that was in 1946, fourteen years earlier, and there were still impediments to overcome in order to register and vote. The first sit-ins in Columbia

From Peaceful Protests to Groundbreaking Rulings

Students picketing a downtown Columbia store. *Courtesy of Cecil Williams.*

were conducted by students from Allen University and Benedict College. One group of students that included Charles Barr, Milton Green, Richard Counts and Johnny Clark sat at the lunch counter at Taylor Street Pharmacy. The second team was Simon Bowie and Talmadge Neal, and they sat at the counter of Eckerd's Drugstore. Both of these actions resulted in lawsuits. The first one was captioned *Charles F. Barr et al v. Taylor Street Pharmacy*, and the second was *Simon Bowie and Talmadge Neal v. Eckerd's Drugstore*. These cases went all the way to the U.S. Supreme Court, which ruled in favor of the plaintiffs. Desegregation of Columbia's lunch counters occurred in 1962. One of the students, Milton Green, would become the first black staffer for U.S. senator Ernest F. Hollings and served in that position for thirteen years.

While the sit-ins were taking place, the Reverend I.D. Newman, now the field secretary for the state NAACP, led a four-mile march through Columbia to the Municipal Airport to desegregate the waiting rooms. Shortly after the airport march, Newman lead a group of divinity students from Allen and Benedict Colleges to challenge the all-white policy at Sesquicentennial State Park. Highway patrolmen headed them off at the park, citing the all-white policy of the State of South Carolina, which said no blacks were allowed in the park. Newman had a hidden tape recorder that documented

Reverend I.D. Newman served as field secretary of the state NAACP from 1960 to 1969. He led many marches and demonstrations during his tenure.

the confrontation. That information enabled attorney Matthew J. Perry to prepare a lawsuit that was heard in U.S. District Court by Judge Robert Martin. He handed down a decision on July 10, 1963, ordering all state parks to desegregate by September 8, 1963. Instead of dropping the barriers, the State Forrest Commission, which operated the parks, ordered all parks closed. After a year of public hearings and behind-the-scenes maneuvering, the parks reopened on June 1, 1964, on a restricted basis. They were fully integrated on July 20, 1966.

Mayor of Columbia Lester Bates did not like the idea of the city being in an unfavorable spotlight. He quietly organized a group of influential blacks and a group of influential whites and began a dialogue that eventually opened the lunch counters to everyone. The black and white signs came down at water fountains and on restroom doors. The community took it all in stride. Eventually, the two groups joined into one under the co-chairmanship of William G. Lisle, a white architect, and Reverend J.M. Hinton, president of the state NAACP. Historians may record this as the turning point of race relations in the city of Columbia. The first undertaking of this group was to set up a training program to prepare young blacks for job opportunities in the white-dominated business community. It was a model program.

Out of these early negotiations, an organization called the Greater Columbia Community Relations Council (GCCRC) was founded. Today, this organization functions as an affiliate of the Greater Columbia Chamber of Commerce and is funded by the City of Columbia and Richland County. The first full-time director was Milton Kimpson. Lincoln C. Jenkins Jr., former school board commissioner, was elected chair of the council. Many other opportunities opened for the black community following the establishment of the GCCRC.

Estelle Trapp Young and Dorothy Jones were among the first to take advantage of these new opportunities when they were appointed parking meter readers. It may sound trivial now, but back then it was a big deal. Tom Elliott, county treasurer, hired the first black employee above janitor when he took on Ben Mack as a tax collector. Mack was Dr. Martin L. King's representative for the SCLC in South Carolina. Elliott then raided the staff of the South Carolina Voter Education Project and hired away Ella Rose Shivers Gladney to be the first white-collar employee in his office in 1968. Elease Boyd would remove the barrier of discrimination in the voter registration office when she became deputy registrar in 1968.

One of the early leaders in Columbia in the 1960s was the Reverend C.J. Whitaker. He was a prominent Baptist Church leader and was very involved in the Richland County Democratic Party for over forty years. He rose through the ranks to vice-chair and then chair of the party. Many aspiring young hopefuls seeking elected office, including I.S. Leevy Johnson, Kay Patterson, Isadore Lourie, Jim Felder, Alex Sanders, John Mason, John Greene, Kirkman Finlay Jr. and many others, sought his advice and counsel as they launched their political careers. Reverend Whitaker lived in the Greenview section of Columbia and was president of the Greenview Precinct, which had over four thousand registered black voters at that time, and during any election, one could expect a 90 percent turnout. In a statewide election, the winner would not be called until the Greenview Precinct votes were in. Reverend Whitaker was affectionately known as the "Budda." It was a name pinned on him by Isadore Lourie, and it stuck.

Another powerful leader in the black community of Columbia was Reverend William McKinley Bowman. He was pastor of the Second Nazareth Baptist Church for over forty years. He was a radio personality and part owner of Radio Station WOIC, which is still on the air but is now owned by others. He was a founding member of the Columbia Branch NAACP and later served on the Richland School District 1 Board for many years.

After George Elmore, Reverend Bowman, Modjeska Simkins, Reverend Whitaker, Ella Rose Gladney, Elease Boyd and Beatrice McKnight knocked down the doors of segregation in Columbia, blacks would walk through and add color to the city and county councils and the school boards. Columbia did not get its first black elected officials until 1970, when Jim Felder and I.S. Leevy Johnson were elected to the South Carolina House of Representatives in a countywide at-large election (the legislators will be discussed in chapter twenty).

In the early 1970s, A.T. Butler won a seat on the Richland County Council. Butler had served as executive director of the Palmetto Education Association (PEA) and was a longtime professor at Allen University. He would later be joined on the council by Willie Rodgers and James L. Solomon. John Roy Harper, the young lawyer who handled many of the single-member district lawsuits, was elected for a short term on the county council. Others who came later to the council included Paul Livingston, Bernice Scott, Cecil Tillis, Thelma Tillis, Damon Jeter, Joyce Dickerson, Gwen Davis Kennedy, Kelvin Washington, Norman Jackson, Harriet Fields, Julius Murray, Gus Roberts, John Scott and Joe McEachern.

Today, blacks in Richland County hold three countywide elected positions. Paul Brawley is the auditor, Jeanette McBride is clerk of court and Dan Johnson is the solicitor for the Fifth Judicial Circuit. At the staff level, Larry Smith is county attorney, and Milton Pope is county administrator. The first black department head was George Wilson, who served as animal control and refuse director.

Richland County has three school districts. School District 1 got its first black board member in 1971, when Dr. Benjamin Payton of Benedict was appointed to the board. When Payton left Columbia to take a position at the Ford Foundation, his unexpired term was completed by J.P. Neal. Lincoln C. Jenkins Jr. followed Neal. Others who would serve include James L. Solomon, Willie Rodgers, Sam Heyward, Reverend William M. Bowman, K.D.B. Jeffcoat, Jasper Salmond, Vince Ford, Damon Jeter, Jamie Devine, Darrell Jackson, Shirley Davis, Jeanette McBride, Leon Howard, Wendy Brawley, Dewayne Smiley, Aaron Bishop, Chris Lindsey and Lavola Taylor. In School District 2, Melinda Anderson, James Price, Sylvia Hannah, Chip Jackson and Regina Corley have served on the board. In School District 5, only one person of color has served on the board in the person of Sherman Anderson.

Columbia City Council did not get its first black members until 1982. That year, a four-two-one plan was approved by the U.S. Justice Department. It provided for the election of four council members from single-member districts and two elected at-large with the mayor. The first blacks elected were Luther Battiste, a graduate of USC and Emory University School of Law, and E.W. Cromartie II, a graduate of the University of Michigan and Howard University School of Law. Cromartie served for twenty-seven years on the council. Sam Davis replaced Battiste on the council, and Tamica Isaac Devine would be the first black to win an at-large seat on the council. Brian DeQuincey Newman replaced Cromartie when he left the council in 2010. Columbia elected its first black mayor, Steve Benjamin, in 2010.

At the staff level in city government, Charles Austin became the first black chief of police. Two other black chiefs followed Austin in the persons of Tandy Carter and Randy Scott. Austin later would become the first black city manager. Aubrey Jenkins is presently the first black fire chief.

Other players in Columbia include Dr. John R. Stevenson, who was the first black superintendent of Richland School District 1. This Allen University graduate served from 1986 to 1994. Frank Washington, another Allen University graduate, was the first black to be employed in a white-collar position with the South Carolina Department of Education, and he worked there for thirty-five years. His first year on the job, he was isolated from whites in the building, as he had to work from a closet. Washington also served as president of the Columbia Branch NAACP for sixteen years.

Durham Carter, another Allen University graduate, was the second person of color to secure a position in state government at the South Carolina Department of Vocational Rehabilitation. He rose through the ranks and became the associate director of that agency. He has lots of stories to tell about the comings and goings of white legislators, governors and U.S. senators at the old Wade Hampton Hotel, where he served as a busboy and hall boy during the early 1950s.

One of the young movers and shakers in Columbia is Heyward Bannister. Born in the lower part of Richland County, this USC graduate was a founding partner and owner of Sunrise Enterprises of Columbia, Inc., a public relations and political consulting firm providing services to corporations and political candidates. In 1992, the Clinton/Gore campaign hired Bannister to serve as its South Carolina state director. Following Clinton's successful run for the White House, Bannister was appointed White House liaison to the U.S. Veterans' Administration, a position he held for six and a half years. Following that assignment, he was named the South Carolina director for Fannie Mae, the federal housing finance agency, where he served from 1999 to 2007.

One of the children of the Columbia movement was Ed Day, who at age eighteen ran for Richland School Board One in 1974. He did not win, but aspiring political candidates took notice and sought his advice on running for public office. Day was a moving force in the petition drive to establish the United Citizen Party (UCP). He was also part of Tom Broadwater's campaign for governor on the UCP ticket in 1970.

One cannot write about Columbia without including the name Redfern. His given name was James Redfern Jr. He dropped the James and became Redfern II, or Deuce, as he was affectionately called. He found an organization called Black On Nation. One of the first black students to attend USC undergraduate school, he became Columbia's most militant activist. He and some of his colleagues held the Richland School District 1 Board of Trustees hostage all night at a school board meeting.

Redfern is best remembered for organizing the largest civil rights demonstration at the state capitol at that time. Some ten thousand marchers gathered at Valley Park, which Redfern renamed Black On Park, for the two-mile march to the capitol. On that cold day in January 1976, these protesters heard speeches from a cross section of people from all over South Carolina. Ralph W. Canty of Sumter presided. Others included Dr. Luns Richardson of Morris College; Bishop D. Ward Nichols of the AME Church; Reverend Matthew McCollom, state president of the NAACP; Dr. W.F. Gibson of Greenville; Willie Williams of Williams & Associates Realty; and Bishop Unterkoffler of the Catholic Diocese of Charleston, the only white person to speak at the rally. The march was billed as a rally to support making Dr. Martin Luther King's birthday a legal holiday, and most of the speakers adhered to that theme. When Redfern took the podium, he delivered a fiery, blistering speech about police brutality and criminal injustice. He leveled a barrage of charges at white public officials, accusing them of defending racist law enforcement officers after they shot down black people. Across the street, on top of the Wade Hampton Hotel, were SLED agents with sniper rifles mounted on tripods; they took aim at Redfern as he ratcheted up his remarks decrying the acts of law enforcement officers. Many in the crowd could feel their hearts racing when they saw those rifles and were very pleased when Redfern finished and was escorted away by bodyguards.

A native Columbian who contributed greatly to healthcare was Dr. Everett Dargan. He returned home after a successful practice in New York and became the first black to serve as chief of staff at Richland Memorial Hospital. The University of South Carolina School of Medicine has endowed a chair in his name for a student entering the medical school.

A milestone for black South Carolinians was the selection of Kimberly Aiken of Columbia as "Miss America" in 1994. The daughter of Charles and Valeria Aiken, she would be only the second person from South Carolina to win the pageant. Marilyn McKnight of Manning, who was white, won it in 1957.

The Columbia Branch NAACP played a major role in diversifying the political process in the capital city. During Adell Adams's tenure as president, the branch pushed for and received U.S. Justice Department approval for single-member districts for county and city council and school board seats. Dr. Lonnie Randolph, an optometrist, followed Adams as both branch president and state conference president. He focused on the removal of the Confederate flag from the dome and the chambers of the senate and House. He led a march of over forty thousand persons to the capitol, the largest crowd of marchers since the Redfern rally in 1976. The flag was removed from the dome and from the chambers of the House and senate. However, it was relocated to the Confederate Monument on the north side of the capitol, facing Gervais Street. The battle to have the flag removed from that location and placed in the Confederate Relic Room continues today. The national NACCP maintains sanctions against the State of South Carolina asking groups and organizations not to hold meetings or conventions in the state until the flag is removed from the capitol grounds.

Credit must be given to Senators Kay Patterson of Columbia and Robert Ford of Charleston, who waged a twenty-year battle in the legislature to have the flag removed. Mayor Bob Coble of Columbia was an ally in the effort to remove the flag. The mayor, who is white, and a coalition of businessmen took the fight to the South Carolina Supreme Court seeking mediation in this matter.

There is a black political dynasty percolating in Columbia. It is the McBride family of Waites Road. This dynasty began when Frank McBride replaced Tom Broadwater in the House of Representatives. Cecil Tillis, Frank's brother-in-law, won a seat on the Richland County Council. Upon his death, his wife, Thelma, Frank's sister, replaced him on the county council. When Thelma retired, her nephew, Damon Jeter, left his Richland School District 1 School Board seat and replaced his aunt on the county council. Frank's wife, Jeannett, replaced nephew Damon on the school board for a term and then ran and won the clerk of court post, where she currently serves. Wilhelmena McBride, Frank's older sister, served on the Wil Lou Gray School Board of Directors for twenty-four years and passed on her seat to her sister, Doris McBride Adams. This seems like a political dynasty in the making. It would seem that any person seeking public office in Richland County should check in with the McBride family.

12

THE CONWAY/MYRTLE BEACH MOVEMENT

U tter the words "Myrtle Beach" anywhere in this country, and in many
places around the world, and the response will be that it is the golf
capital of the world. There are more golf courses in this one location than
in any other place in the world. It has more usable beachfront than any
other state except Florida. Millions of tourists visit the beach each year from
around the world. Utter the words "Myrtle Beach" to blacks who have lived
in the area for the last two or three generations, and they will remind you of
another time when it was a segregated place.

Beginning in the 1930s, blacks worked on Myrtle Beach as cooks,
drivers, maids and grass cutters but could not use the beach for recreational
purposes. Jim Crow laws of the time would not allow blacks to swim in
the ocean alongside whites. They could not use the state park, which was
located there, either. In 1933, a man named George Tyson took an option
on a piece of property that later would become Atlantic Beach. When Tyson
ran into financial difficulty, Dr. Peter Kelly of Conway led an effort to find
some doctors, college presidents and other black professionals to jointly pool
the funds needed to form the Atlantic Beach Company. Dr. Robert Gordon
of Dillon built a two-story hotel at the corner of Atlantic Street and Ocean
Drive and named it the Gordon Hotel. Atlantic Beach then became the
place for families to go for swimming, dancing, playing in the ocean and
having a good time.

Some of the early businesses on Atlantic Beach were the Marshal Hotel,
Blue Bird Inn, the Patio and the Rainbow Inn. There were several clubs and
restaurants, a movie house, a grocery store and two liquor stores. Amusement

rides included a Ferris wheel and merry-go-round, which pleased the youngsters very much. There was the Cotton Club, Atlantic Beach's first outdoor pavilion, and it hosted top entertainers. On any given night, James Brown, the Tams, the Drifters, Ray Charles, Martha & the Vandellas and many others might show up. These showmen would play at the white clubs on Myrtle Beach in the early evenings and come to Atlantic Beach and jam into the early morning hours. Bus- and truckloads of blacks came from as far away as Columbia, Orangeburg and Sumter during the season when the beach was open.

Atlantic Beach thrived until 1954, when Hurricane Hazel destroyed many of the businesses, homes and hotels. Many owners did not have insurance and did not rebuild. After the passage of the 1964 Civil Rights Act doing away with segregation in public facilities, Atlantic Beach fell on hard times. A visit there today is like a step back in time. Many of the old places are still there in run-down condition, some boarded up and others just a shell of what they once were.

In 1966, the town was incorporated and elected its first mayor and council. A town hall was built, and a fire department was formed. Senator Strom Thurmond helped secure a grant from the HUD that was used to build some affordable housing and a community center. In recent years, many efforts have been made to develop the town by outside developers, but the local landowners refused to cooperate.

Atlantic Beach began hosting a bike festival in recent years, hoping to bring in thousands of dollars to support the local economy.

In an effort to integrate Myrtle Beach in the early 1960s, Reverend I.D. Newman, field secretary of the state NAACP, led a group to the beach to stage a "wade-in." Two cars of blacks and one white attempted to enter Myrtle Beach State Park. Upon arrival, they were denied permission to enter. Chief J.P. Strom of SLED and plain-clothed police officers told him that the park was closed and could not accept any more visitors. The incident led to a class-action lawsuit known as *J. Arthur Brown v. South Carolina Forrest Commission*. Brown was president of the state NAACP and a native of Charleston. The case was heard by U.S. District Court judge J. Robert Martin, and on July 10, 1963, he issued an order desegregating the state park system in South Carolina.

Following Newman and company's attempt to desegregate Myrtle Beach, he had to flee for his life as the KKK chased him out of Horry County. Newman's efforts galvanized the black community of Conway and Myrtle Beach. The Horry County Progressive League was organized, and it registered over two thousand black voters and began to flex its political muscles. Myrtle Beach elected its first black city councilman, James Futrell, in 1980. In 1992, Ralph Wilson of Conway would be elected solicitor for that circuit, becoming the first solicitor of color in South Carolina. He served until 2000.

Years following desegregation of the beaches, Conway and Myrtle Beach would be in the spotlight in a negative way because of an incident at Conway High School. In 1989, the coach at the school replaced the black quarterback with a white player, and the other black players refused to play and started a strike. The strike was also in protest of the suspension of Reverend H.H. Singleton, a teacher in the Horry County School System. Reverend Singleton was president of the Conway NAACP and supported the players' strike. The state NAACP entered the flap and shifted its monthly board meeting from Columbia to Myrtle Beach, dubbing the event "Preach on the Beach" Saturday. Benjamin Hooks, national executive director of the NAACP; Dr. William F. Gibson, chair of the NAACP national board; and other leaders from around South Carolina rallied to Singleton's cause. Singleton was later reinstated with back pay. Conway and Myrtle Beach then held mediation sessions with the NAACP to correct deficiencies in the hiring practices by commercial and government entities in Horry County.

In an effort to preserve black life and history in Horry County, Professor O'Neal Smalls of the University of South Carolina Law School founded Freewoods Farm in the Burgess Community near Myrtle Beach. The objective of Freewoods is to replicate the way farming was done on small animal- and human-powered farms in South Carolina between the Civil War and 1900. While the primary focus is on black-operated farms, it will apply to all small family farms in the state during that period. The public will be able to see history in action by visiting the farm. To ensure the historical accuracy of the project, a major research project, "Operation Reach Back," was done by a joint team of researchers from South Carolina State University, the University of South Carolina and Clemson University.

The farm is becoming an attraction for tourists visiting the area. The founder, O'Neal Smalls, is a descendant of Sye Smalls, who was a newly freed slave in 1864 when he obtained a small tract of land along the Waccamah River in Horry County and began to farm it. O'Neal Smalls serves as president of Freewoods Farm Foundation. He is a graduate of Tuskegee University and earned law degrees from Harvard and Georgetown Universities. He was one of the first black professors at USC Law School. Detailed information on Freewoods Farm can be found at freewoodsfarm.com.

13

THE FLORENCE/DARLINGTON MOVEMENT

The city of Florence is the county seat for Florence County. It has been called the "Queen City" of the Pee Dee area of the state. Many passenger and freight trains pass through the city daily, and it has become a railroad hub for the Atlantic Coast Line Railroad and, later, AMTRAC and CSX Railroad. In the early years, tobacco was the mainstay in Florence. Persons traveling north and south on U.S. Highway 301 know of Sexton Dental Clinic, a twenty-four-hour, seven-day-a-week operation that provided care for the teeth of thousands of individuals from up and down the East Coast. In recent years, Florence's economy shifted heavily to healthcare. Two major providers of healthcare, McLeod Regional Medical Center and Carolinas Hospital System, serve persons from throughout the Pee Dee area. They employ thousands of individuals. Some pharmaceutical companies have set up manufacturing plants in the area. With the establishment of Francis Marion College, Florence has become a college town.

In the black community Dr. R.N. Beck was a leading provider of healthcare, as well as an activist in civil rights. His office was a minor medical clinic, where he provided health services that blacks could not receive at the old Florence Hospital. A native of Georgetown, Dr. Beck was the chairman of the South Carolina Voter Education Project's Sixth Congress District activities. In the early years, during the 1940s and 1950s, he was active in the Progressive Democratic Party. Up until his death in 2003, he was still an activist and a voice for the voiceless in Florence.

Another soldier in the war for equality in Florence was Reverend William P. Diggs, pastor of Trinity Baptist Church. It was at his church that many of the civil rights rallies and meetings were held. There were not a lot of marches and demonstrations in Florence because there were no college students to draw from for such activities. However, some high school students did participate in some sit-ins in local department stores.

There were no black elected officials in Florence until Mordai Johnson, a native of the area, returned home and became the first city council member. He was a graduate of Morris College, held law degrees from Howard University and George Washington University and had served as a member of the U.S. Commission on Civil Rights. Johnson sang and played the piano in Washington, D.C., to earn money to pay his expenses for law school. He ran for the South Carolina House of Representatives on two occasions without success, but he became Florence's first black municipal court judge. He was a prolific writer, and his column appeared in the *Pee Dee Times*, the *Charleston Chronicle*, *Jet* and *Ebony* magazines and other papers around the country.

Jerry Keith, a local businessman in Florence, became the first black to be elected to the Florence County Council. After reapportionment of the General Assembly, Maggie Glover would represent Florence, first in the House of Representatives and later in the state senate. Frank Gilbert also would serve in the state senate. In later years, Mack Hines and Terry Alexander represented Florence in the House of Representatives.

Next door to Florence is Darlington, which is like a twin city because of its proximity; it is known for the "Southern 500" NASCAR race. This race ran annually from 1950 until 2004, when NASCAR moved its national headquarters away from Darlington.

The early leaders in the Darlington movement were Mann Stanley, W.J. Hunter and David Pugh. All three were businessmen, and they led the civil rights activities in the area. Stanley owned and operated a service station on the south end of Main Street and headed the Darlington NAACP. David Pugh sold musical instruments to black high schools throughout the state. He also led a band that played for many of the social functions around the state. Hunter operated a grocery store on the north end of Main Street just south of the main business district. He was labeled at one point by the white power structure as the most dangerous black man in South Carolina because of his involvement with the Progressive Democratic Party. On a visit to his store, one would find him wearing a stingy brim hat with a cigar in the corner of his mouth. He was one of the founders of the Progressive Democratic Party and was a target of the KKK.

Stanley's efforts to desegregate Darlington's public schools began in the early 1960s, and it took over thirty years, until 1994, before his lawsuit was finally resolved. His early actions resulted in the school board adopting a midyear integration plan in the small town of Lamar, which created attendance zones. The plan resulted in the creation of one high school for majority whites and a second high school for majority blacks and some poor whites. On opening day of school, some angry whites attacked a bus carrying black students and overturned it. Some of the children were injured, and the mob attacked the highway patrolmen who had been sent by Governor McNair to maintain order. A lot of the blame for this was placed on Congressman Albert Watson, who had been an advocate for freedom of choice. Watson was running for governor and had addressed an audience in Darlington and whipped up the crowd by stating, "Every section of this state is in for it unless you stand up and use every means at your disposal to defend what I consider an illegal order from the U.S. Circuit Court of Appeals." Watson did not win the governor's race. John West was the victor, and he began serving as a new breed of southern governors. The members of the mob were convicted by an all-white jury for attacking the bus and highway patrolmen. Years later, Robert Grooms was elected mayor of Lamar, becoming the first black to hold this office.

Other black elected officials in Darlington County include Wilhelmena P. Johnson on the county council and Gerald Malloy, the first black state senator from Darlington. At the school board level, Charles Govan would be elected chairman of the Hartsville School Board.

With the doors now open, many others would be elected to the city and county councils, school boards and other positions in Florence and Darlington Counties.

14

THE GREENVILLE MOVEMENT

The beginning of the Greenville movement can be traced back to December 1959, when native son Jesse Jackson came home for the Christmas holidays from the University of Illinois, where he was a freshman. He needed to use the public library for preparing a term paper project. When he attempted to enter, two policemen barred his way. He vowed he would return. The next year, he did return. However, before he could keep his vow, a group of students in 1960 walked inside the all-white Greenville Public Library, and when they refused to leave, they were arrested.

Later that month, Doris D. Wright, who was a fifteen-year-old student at Sterling High School and president of the NAACP Youth Council, returned with other students. This time, when the students refused to leave, the library closed its doors. The advisor to the students was Reverend James Hall, pastor of Springfield Baptist Church. He was respected in the black community, and he served as second vice-president of the Greenville Branch NAACP. Each time the students were denied permission to use the library, he counseled and encouraged them to keep trying.

On July 16, 1960, the students met with Reverend Hall at his church to plan yet another attempt to desegregate the public library. This group was called the "Greenville 8," and it included Joan Mattison Daniel, Elaine Means, Margaree Seabrook, Doris D. Wright, Hattie Smith, Jesse Jackson, Benjamin Downs and Willie Joe Wright. Upon entering the library, the group was arrested. The eight were taken to the police station and booked. The lawyers for this group were Donald Sampson and Willie T. Smith. They immediately filed a lawsuit in the U.S. District Court. On September 2,

1960, the Greenville Public Library was closed and reopened on September 19, 1960, as an integrated facility.

After the "Greenville 8" incident, Dorris D. Wright and her fellow NAACP Youth Council members focused on integrating all public facilities in Greenville. They participated in sit-ins at Woolworth, S.H. Kress and other department stores in downtown Greenville that maintained segregated lunch counters and water fountains. They also set out to integrate public parks. When they attempted to integrate the public swimming pools, the city council covered up the pools and made flower gardens out of them. They focused on the churches. Wright and her youth council members tried to attend worship services at the church that the mayor attended. They were denied admittance. Wright said to the usher at the door, "Christ came once, and he was refused. How do you know that he is not coming in the form of a Negro?" This must have touched a nerve, for on the next Sunday, the students were allowed to worship.

The students of the early Greenville movement would go on to make their marks in other parts of the United States. Jesse would join Dr. Martin Luther King and the SCLC and later founded Operation PUSH in Chicago; he also would run twice for president of the United States. Margaree Seabrook married Willis Crosby, and both earned doctorate degrees at the University of Massachusetts at the same time. Margaree would become the first black female professor at Clemson University. Willis would head the Greenville Community Action Agency, SHARE, for over twenty-five years. Dorris D. Wright broke

Students are turned away from an all-white church. *Courtesy of Cecil Williams.*

the glass ceiling at Clark College and became the first female president of the Student Government Association. Later, she earned a master's in social work from the University of Missouri and became an activist in Salisbury, North Carolina, where she serves on many boards and commissions.

While the sit-ins, wade-ins and pray-ins were going on, A.J. Whittenburg, president of the Greenville NAACP, and several other parents took a request to the Greenville School Board asking that six black students, including Whittenburg's daughter, be allowed to transfer to white schools. The request was denied, and the parents filed a lawsuit in the federal district court. The court ruled in their favor in 1964, and fifty-five black students enrolled in sixteen white schools. Paul Pepper and L.R. Bird were two of those students. In later years, Bird would serve as a consultant to the national NAACP and direct the organization's "Fair Share" project. He became a radio personality and hosted an afternoon talk show for many years.

Greenville was placed in the national spotlight in 1959, when Jackie Robinson, the first black person to play major-league baseball with the Brooklyn Dodgers in 1947, was threatened with arrest after he refused to leave the white waiting room at the Greenville Airport. This incident was followed by marches and protests at the airport led by Reverend James Hall. The airport removed the signs marked "colored" and "white" shortly thereafter, and the airport was no longer segregated.

During the period from 1960 to 1962, clashes often erupted on Greenville streets between whites and the student protestors. Curfews were imposed, and tensions mounted. Students were frequently arrested and confined in the city jail for breaking local segregation laws. When the protestors strained the confines of the city jail, they were transferred to the county stockade until bail could be posted. On June 3, 1963, a week after the Greenville City Council removed all of the city's segregation laws from the books following the U.S. Supreme Court's ruling in *Peterson v. the State of South Carolina*, blacks were served food and drinks at eleven stores in Greenville. This would be the beginning of the end of segregation at all public facilities in Greenville.

In 1969, Dr. W.F. Gibson, a local dentist, organized a group called the Black Council for Progress (BCP). The purpose of the group was to promote advocacy in the black community. This group served to remind the community that the battle for civil and equal rights was not won. Others in the group included S.T. Peden, Harrison Reardon, Andrew Chisholm, Tommy Hagood, Joe Vaughn, Bulah Channel, Peggie Parks, James Epps, Stan Williams, Dr. Steve Moore, Sherwood Thompson, Harnetha Smith, Willis Crosby and Reverend Martin England. Dr. Gibson would go on to become president of the state NAACP and national board chairman of the NAACP. Andrew Chisholm campaigned for President Jimmy Carter and was rewarded by Carter in 1977 with the appointment to U.S. marshal for South Carolina, a first in the state.

Greenville's two black lawyers, Donald Sampson and Willie T. Smith, were joined by three other young black lawyers, Theo W. Mitchell, John Bishop and Isaac Joe, in 1972. Other black barristers would come: Andrew Jones, Mike Talley, James A. Duckett, Tee Ferguson, Lawrence T. Acker, Dorothy Manigault, Alex Kinlaw, Margaret Mills, Merl F. Code, Robert Jenkins, Fletcher Smith, William J. Weston, Julliette Mims, Donna Mosely and Ernest Hamilton.

Blacks in Greenville began running for public office in 1963, when Donald Sampson ran unsuccessfully for the House of Representatives. In the 1970s, there would be successful candidates at various levels. On the city council, Dr. E.L. McPherson, Reverend Rafield Metcalf, J.D. Mathis, Lillian Brock Fleming and Ralph Anderson were successful. At the county council level, Bishop Johnny Smith, Ennis Fant and Reverend E.D. Dixon were elected. Later, Lottie B. Gibson and Leola Robinson served on the county council. Theo W. Mitchell and Sara Shelton were elected to the House of Representatives, and later Mitchell moved on to the South Carolina Senate. There would be many blacks appointed to county and city boards and commissions.

A strong force in Greenville was Alberta T. Grimes. She chaired the commission that received the first Head Start grant in South Carolina. She served as president of the Palmetto Education Association. She was one of the first two blacks to serve on the University of South Carolina Board of Trustees.

Lenny F. Springs, an Edgefield native who pursued a career in banking, spent time in Greenville and contributed much to the involvement of blacks in the business of Greenville. He served on the NAACP Special Board of Trustees. He is an advisor to President Barack Obama and the U.S. Department of Education. A graduate of Voorhees College, he sits on its board of trustees.

There were others who played strategic roles in the Greenville movement. There was Mark Talbert, who served as vice-president of the local NAACP during Whittenberg's tenure. The two of them led many protests and demonstrations. Fred Garrett, a farm extension agent for the county and school district, ultimately became a mortician and developed the largest black-owned funeral home in Greenville—Watkins-Garrett-Woods. During the 1950s, when he was a government employee, he had to keep his NAACP membership secret because the state had outlawed membership in the organization. To get around this problem, government employees were issued membership cards with numbers on them instead of the individuals' names. Garrett's number was 6-N. He has become the "Godfather" of black politics in Greenville and still spends some time in his office at the funeral home, where his children operate the business these days.

Dr. Thomas C. Kerns became the first black superintendent of schools for Greenville County. Greenville is a white-majority county with an eighty-to-twenty ratio white to black. In 1984, Kerns was named interim superintendent and later superintendent, where he served until retirement.

A person who was noted for his musical skills was Moses Dillard. He had a musical group named the Textile Display, and it traveled throughout the Southeast providing entertainment. He was very involved in the politics of Greenville. Today, his daughter, Shandra Dillard, serves in the South Carolina House of Representatives. Dillard played a major role in developing the talent of the singer Pebo Bryson.

When the Urban League came to Greenville, it brought Bill Whitney from Columbia to get it up and running. Whitney was a product of the Columbia Urban League; he served as president/CEO of the Greenville League for many years and was very involved in community activities.

In the Greenville judicial system, Fletcher N. Smith broke new ground when he was appointed assistant solicitor in 1980, becoming the first black to hold such a position in the Thirteenth Judicial Circuit. Smith later was elected to the South Carolina House of Representatives.

A mentor to many athletes in Greenville, including Jesse Jackson, was coach J.D. Mathis. He coached at Sterling High School and won many state championships during the 1950s and 1960s.

Finally, there was Sam Zimmerman, who recorded much of the changes and progress in Greenville. He is the author of *Negroes in Greenville* and *Desegregation: A Model Plan*. He won many awards as director of school/communication relations for the school district.

15

THE ORANGEBURG MOVEMENT

Located forty miles south of Columbia is Orangeburg, the seat of Orangeburg County. It is a rural agriculture community and home to two HBCU learning institutions, Claflin University and South Carolina State University, the only public black state-supported higher education school in the state. The movement in Orangeburg can be divided into five phases.

The first phase was in 1955, when blacks in Orangeburg sought to integrate the public school system. Following the *Brown v. Board of Education* decision, it was the thinking that all schools would automatically desegregate. That did not happen. After many meetings, the NAACP branch in Orangeburg decided to petition the school board to admit its children. Signatures were gathered on petitions for presentation to the school board. Instead of responding to the parents, the white community formed a "White Citizens Council" and published the names of those parents who signed the petition. Immediately, retaliation was leveled at the signers. Some lost their jobs. Others were refused credit by white merchants. Home deliveries were halted for products like milk and ice. Banks and mortgage companies called in loans for immediate payment.

The local NAACP president, Reverend Matthew McCollom, called a meeting to deal with the situation. The NAACP decided to retaliate against the merchants with a boycott of all white-owned stores. Blacks would travel as far as Columbia and Charleston to do their shopping. Though inconvenient for many in the community, the boycott was successful. The White Citizens Council and the white merchants backed off the tactics they were employing against the black community. The leaders of this first phase

The steering committee of the Orangeburg Freedom Movement. *From left to right*: Reverend Matthew W. McCollom, James E. Sulton, Dr. Harlowe E. Caldwell, Constance Baker-Motley, John E. Brunson, Lincoln C. Jenkins Esq., Gloria Rackley, J. Arthur Brown and Dr. Charles E. Thomas. *Courtesy of Cecil Williams.*

of the movement, in addition to Reverend McCollom, were James Sulton, treasurer of the NAACP; Reverend Francis Donlon, a white Catholic priest and secretary of the NAACP; and John Brunson.

During this period, Thurgood Marshall, chief counsel for the national NAACP, visited Orangeburg on November 27, 1955, and addressed a mass meeting on the campus of Claflin University. Some 1,500 persons turned out to hear Marshall update them on the status of the Brown decision. It would be one of many mass meetings held throughout South Carolina featuring the big man from the NAACP legal department.

The second phase of the movement occurred in 1956, when students staged a strike on the campus of South Carolina State College. Fred Moore of Charleston was the SGA president. He presented a list of grievances to Dr. B.C. Turner, president of the college. The number one concern was the purchasing of goods and services from white merchants who were members of the White Citizens Council for use on campus. Turner denied the request, and a five-day student strike ensued. Of the more than 1,200 students on campus, all participated except the law school students, graduate students and elementary students in Felton Laboratory. This was the students' way of showing the outside community that they supported the efforts it was using to eliminate segregation in Orangeburg.

From Peaceful Protests to Groundbreaking Rulings

Fred Moore would pay a supreme price for his leadership in this struggle. The boycott took place in February 1956. On April 25, 1956, two weeks prior to graduation, senior class member Fred Moore was expelled for leading an "insurrection" on campus, according to President Turner and the all-white board of trustees. Allen University in Columbia took Moore in the following year, and he was allowed to graduate with the Allen University class of 1957. Omega Psi Phi fraternity provided scholarship funds for Moore to attend Howard University School of Law. He graduated from law school and returned to Charleston, where he practiced law for many years. Currently, he is a bishop in the Reform Episcopal Church.

The third phase of the movement occurred on March 16, 1960, when over 1,500 students marched from the campus to downtown Orangeburg and staged sit-ins at Kress and other department stores. This would be the largest student demonstration thus far during the sit-ins from a black college campus. Jim Clyburn, a student at South Carolina State, was a leader in that movement. After being jailed, he met his future wife, Emily England, behind bars. Those marches and demonstrations continued for the next two years. Back on campus, President Turner had no interest in supporting the student movement, and he discouraged students from participating. He expelled some students for their participation.

Ministers and others marching in Orangeburg in 1963. *Courtesy of Cecil Williams.*

The fourth phase of the movement focused on the ouster of President Turner. In February 1967, some ten years after Charleston native Fred Moore was expelled from South Carolina State for leading demonstrations, another Charleston native, Ike Williams, followed in Moore's footsteps and led another demonstration on campus. This demonstration was triggered by the refusal of the administration to consider a long list of grievances. Included on the list were class cuts, campus attire, attendance at vesper services and the decision by the administration not to renew two white professors' contracts whose Woodrow Wilson Fellowships had expired. President Turner did not address these concerns, and after two weeks of demonstrations, Ike Williams, Alexander Nichols, Johnny Bishop and Robert Cunningham made a trip to Columbia and met with Governor Robert E. McNair. They asked the governor to fire President Turner. After much discussion with the students, McNair asked Turner to resign. On May 5, 1967, the board of trustees accepted Turner's resignation. This boycott and demonstration were known as "The Cause."

This meeting between Ike Williams and McNair would be the beginning

of a relationship that would last for the lifetimes of both men. Both are now deceased. Ike became what one might call a "Godchild" of McNair. Ike graduated from South Carolina State's ROTC program as a second lieutenant and served his country for two years. He returned to South Carolina in 1969 and accepted the position of field secretary of the state NAACP. He left that assignment to join Congressman Jim Clyburn's staff, a position he held until his death on February 15, 2008.

In fairness to Dr. B.C. Turner, he made some accomplishments during his tenure at South Carolina State. He guided the institution into membership in the SACS

Isaac W. Williams served as field secretary for the state NAACP for fourteen years. As a student at South Carolina State College, he led the movement that led to the resignation of President B.C. Turner in 1967.

(Southern Association of Colleges and Schools). Some twenty-three buildings were erected on campus. Turner was an introvert and built a wall between him and the faculty and students. He totally ignored the outside community.

Up until 1966, the South Carolina State Board of Trustees was an all-white body. Its first blacks were appointed in 1966 in the persons of I.P. Stanback of Columbia and Dr. James Boykins of Lancaster. Later, the board would become a majority-black male body until Jackie Gilmore became the first female to serve on the board. Today, there is one white male on the board.

The fifth phase of the movement began in January 1968, when students sought admission to a bowling alley in the downtown area. Orangeburg would find itself in the national spotlight when, on February 8, 1968, South Carolina highway patrolmen fired shotguns into a crowd of students who were gathered on the front lawn of the campus of South Carolina State. Three students were killed and twenty-seven others injured. This event became known as the Orangeburg Massacre. All of the students killed or injured were shot in the back as they retreated up the hill. This incident grew out of the demonstrations taking place at the All-Star Bowling Lanes, which had an "all-white policy" that prevented blacks from using the facility.

Dr. Oscar Butler, dean of students at South Carolina State College, raises his hand in a request for students to calm themselves in their attempt to integrate the All-Star Bowling Lanes in Orangeburg. *Courtesy of Cecil Williams.*

This is a scene from a memorial service on the campus of South Carolina State University for the victims of the Orangeburg Massacre. *Courtesy of Cecil Williams.*

Authors Jack Bass and Jack Nelson chronicle the events of that evening in their book, *The Orangeburg Massacre*. This event did not get a lot of coverage at the time. There were other events such as the assassinations of Dr. Martin King and Robert Kennedy, and the Vietnam War was tearing the country apart. There were campus uprising at USC-Berkley and Columbia University. There were killings at Kent State and Jackson State.

There was no apology from the State of South Carolina for the massacre at Orangeburg until 2001, when Governor Jim Hodges expressed his regrets on behalf of the state at the annual memorial service in Orangeburg for the slain and injured students. In 2003, Governor Mark Sanford issued an apology—finally.

During all of these movements in Orangeburg, there was great leadership in the black community. In addition to those cited above, there were J.I. Washington Jr., Reverend J. Herbert Nelson, Dr. Charles Thomas, Oscar P. Butler, Reverend Roland, Tom Moss, Lucky Adams, Earl Middleton, lawyers Newton Pugh and Zack Townsend and many others.

The fruits from the labor of these movements propelled blacks to run for public office. Roger Cleckley, a Vietnam veteran, has served as county auditor for the past thirty years. Samuetta Marshall, black and female, is coroner. Larry Williams served as sheriff. John Rickenbacher served as chair of the county council. Liz Keitt and Bernard Hare took seats on the Orangeburg City Council. Silas Seabrook would serve as mayor of Santee for over twenty years. Colonel Richard Singleton, a 1958 ROTC graduate of South Carolina State and a native of Sumter, returned to Orangeburg and became the first public safety director when that position was created.

Orangeburg began sending black legislators to the statehouse in 1974 in the persons of Larry Mitchell, John W. Matthews, Earl Middleton, Ken Bailey, Gilda Cobb-Hunter and Jerry Govan.

16

THE ROCK HILL MOVEMENT

In 1957, Rock Hill was a town of thirty thousand people, of whom twenty thousand were white and ten thousand were black. It is the home of two HBCUs: Clinton Junior College, supported by the African Methodist Episcopal Zion Church, and Friendship Junior College, supported by the Baptist Education and Missionary Convention. Located in the northern part of South Carolina, twenty miles south of Charlotte, North Carolina, Rock Hill's industry was textile and domestic workers. On a hot July day in 1957, Rock Hill would be propelled into the national spotlight by a spontaneous bus boycott staged by black residents. This was the beginning of several movements in Rock Hill.

The boycott began after Addelene Austin White wanted a seat on a Rock Hill city bus. A white woman offered to allow her to sit next to her, but the driver intervened and told White she could not sit next to the white woman. White told the driver to stop the bus and let her off because she was not going to stand that day. Once off the bus, she walked three miles to her home. She was angry, and she talked to herself all the way home that afternoon. Her action put her right up there with Rosa Parks of Alabama and Sarah Mae Flemming of Eastover, South Carolina, two other women who challenged segregated bus seating in the 1950s.

Word of the incident spread fast in Rock Hill, where over six hundred blacks rode the bus each day, and they just stopped riding. Before the Rock Hill NAACP Branch could organize a demonstration and march, the community just stopped supporting the Star Bus Lines and Taxi Company. A week following the incident, Reverend C.A. Ivory, president of the local

NAACP, called a meeting of his legal team, and they began to plan an extended boycott of the bus line. Reverend Ivory was six-foot-six and served as pastor of the Hermon Presbyterian Church in Rock Hill. A childhood injury had left him confined to a wheelchair, from which he directed the boycott from his front porch. He kept a cane in his lap and a shotgun behind the door. He received threats from the KKK and White Citizens Council members, but it did not deter him. Matthew J. Perry, then a young lawyer practicing in Spartanburg, came to Rock Hill to assist in the legal aspects of the matter. The boycott continued for some four years. Reverend Ivory and other ministers in Rock Hill organized a car pool and purchased a couple station wagons to transport workers to their jobs during that four-year period.

As for Addelene Austin White, she left Rock Hill and relocated to New York City seeking better job opportunities. She never discussed the matter or the role she played in starting this boycott with her family or friends. It was only in the 1990s that she would discuss it. She said she loved Rock Hill and continued to return for family gatherings every September. Now she is more than just a footnote in history; she is a hero of the civil rights movement.

In 1960, as the bus boycott was rocking along, some students from Friendship Junior College and Clinton Junior College staged a sit-in at the Woolworth and McCrory stores in downtown Rock Hill on February 12, 1960. They were arrested, taken before a magistrate, fined and released. This would go on for almost a year. On January 31, 1961, the Rock Hill movement would take its exercise to a new level. Instead of accepting a bond and being released, some of the students decided to stay in jail. It became the "Jail No Bail" movement. It started when nine students from Friendship Junior College decided to accept thirty-day sentences of hard labor on the chain gang rather than be released. The "Friendship Nine," as they would become known, were led by a student name John Gaines. They were supported by a young man name Tom Gaither. Gaither was a field secretary for CORE, and he trained them for the mission. Assisting the Friendship Nine in their legal matters was Ernest A. Finney Jr., then a young lawyer practicing in Sumter and serving as counsel for CORE. Another advisor for this group was James T. McCain of Sumter, who served as regional director for CORE. In 1962, after many sit-ins and demonstrations by college and high school students, Rock Hill quietly desegregated its lunch counters.

On May 20, 2011, the state NAACP honored the Friendship Nine at its annual Freedom Fund Celebration in Columbia. Those brave nine students included John Gaines, who was a graduate of Emmett Scott High School in Rock Hill, spent two years at Friendship Junior College and earned a bachelor's degree from Benedict College. He earned his law degree from Howard University and returned to South Carolina, where he practiced law in Rock Hill and Florence. He handled many of the civil rights cases that made their way to the U.S. Supreme Court and effected change in the political process.

Thomas Gaither, the only member of the Friendship Nine who was not a Rock Hill native and did not attend either of the colleges in Rock Hill, was raised twenty miles down the road in Great Falls, South Carolina. He graduated from Claflin College in Orangeburg. Following a stint in the U.S. Army, he became a professor of biology and taught at Slippery Rock College for over thirty years.

Clarence Graham, a graduate of the Emmett Scott High class of 1959, served in the U.S. Air Force and worked for the State of South Carolina for over twenty years.

Willie T. Massey, a graduate of the Emmett Scott High class of 1960, attended Clinton Junior College and Johnson C. Smith University. After military service, he earned a master's degree from Winthrop University and taught school and served as a guidance counselor in York County. He served as a pastor in the York County area.

Willie McLeod was a member of the Emmett Scott High class of 1960. He was active in the early sit-ins and coordinated training for nonviolent direct action before and after his experience with the Friendship Nine. He served in the U.S. Army and returned to Rock Hill. For two decades, he ran his own business, Willie's Grading & Lawn Service.

James Wells, a 1959 graduate of Emmett Scott High School, spent his first year at South Carolina State College. After graduating from Friendship Junior College, he enlisted in the U.S. Air Force. After his military obligation, he enrolled in John C. Smith University and later completed law school at the University of Illinois.

David Williamson Jr. was part of the Emmett Scott High School class of 1960 and matriculated to Friendship Junior College. He later moved to New Jersey but returned to Rock Hill and worked in education in Charlotte and Rock Hill schools.

Mack Workman, a member of the Emmett Scott School class of 1960, attended Friendship Junior College and moved to New York City, where he worked in Social Services advising troubled youth, including those who were in prison.

Each of these individuals received the NAACP Civil Rights Advocacy Award. The speaker for the occasion was the U.S. attorney for South Carolina, Bill Nettles.

From Peaceful Protests to Groundbreaking Rulings

In May 1961, the Freedom Riders passed through Rock Hill. James Farmer, the founder of CORE, and other black and white riders boarded a bus in Washington, D.C., to test interstate travel in the South. One of the stops was in Rock Hill. The purpose of this venture was to eliminate segregated waiting rooms and bathrooms in bus terminals. The bus's destination was New Orleans. In Rock Hill, some of the riders were jailed for a period of time. Ernest A. Finney, CORE's lawyer, was pulled out of a social function in Sumter by James T. McCain and hustled up to Rock Hill to defend some of the riders who had been jailed. These riders included John Lewis, later Congressman Lewis of Georgia; Diane Nash, leader of the Nashville Student Movement; Hank Thomas; Reverend C.T. Vivian; Bernard Lafette; and others who were detained until Finney could work things out.

There was never a shortage of good leadership in Rock Hill. In addition to Reverend Ivory, there was Dr. Dewey Duckett Sr., a past president of the local NAACP and a practicing physician in Rock Hill. There was Dr. Horace Goggins, a dentist and secretary of the NAACP. In later years, Juanita Goggins, wife of Dr. Goggins, would become the first black female to be elected to the South Carolina House of Representatives in 1974. She served three terms or six years. Her other first was an appointment to the U.S. Civil Rights Commission. She was twice invited to the White House by President Jimmy Carter. Tragically, she was found frozen to death in February 2010. She was living alone, and dementia had begun to set in.

Sam Foster replaced Goggins in the legislature. He served until he was elected a commissioner on the Employment Security Commission by his fellow legislators. Bessie Moody-Lawrence replaced Foster in the House of Representatives, and upon her retirement, John King took that seat representing House District 49.

17

THE SPARTANBURG MOVEMENT

L ocated in the north-central part of South Carolina, Spartanburg is noted
for textiles and peaches. Although Georgia calls itself the Peach State,
more peaches are grown in Spartanburg County than in all of Georgia.
Spartanburg is the home of Arthur Prysock, the singer, and his brother,
Red Prysock, a big band leader of the 1950s and '60s. The modern-day
movement in Spartanburg began with the sit-ins in 1960. Two high school
students, George Foster and his buddy Big Boy Campbell, staged a sit-in at
the Woolworth's lunch counter on July 27, 1960, launching the protests in
this city.

The night before this daring action by these teenagers, there was a
planning meeting by the adults, and the decision was made to do a sit-in.
However, later in the evening, the protest was cancelled and would be done
at another time. No one told Foster and Campbell about the postponement,
and the next day they went downtown. No one showed up, and after waiting
for a while, they decided to sit at the Woolworth's lunch counter. The police
arrested them and placed them in jail. Matthew J. Perry, Spartanburg's only
black lawyer at the time, represented the students, and they were released in
a matter of hours. Their action shocked the black community into action.
There would be more sit-ins and demonstrations for the next two and a half
years, until the city desegregated its lunch counters in 1963.

In Spartanburg, South Liberty Street was the heart of the black business
district. Most of the services needed by the black community could be found
on South Liberty. There was Bull's Clinic, owned and operated by Dr. J.C.
Bull. It was more than a doctor's office. He had beds there for overnight stays
for those with serious illnesses. It really was a mini hospital. Next door to
the clinic was Oliver's Drugstore, owned and operated by pharmacist Eddie

From Peaceful Protests to Groundbreaking Rulings

Oliver. Just down the street were Collins Funeral Home, Collins Hotel and Collins Taxi Services. North Carolina Mutual Life Insurance Company had an office on Liberty, and so did lawyer Matthew J. Perry. For great barbecue, there was Sarge's Place. Charles Atchison Checker Cab Company was on Liberty Street. There were many other mom-and-pop shops and restaurants on Liberty. A black person only went downtown for banking and to mail letters and packages.

Ministers in Spartanburg provided needed leadership. There were Reverend Harold Cox and Reverend C.M. Johnson leading the ministers. Roy Henderson provided leadership from the NAACP. In addition to their medical practice, Dr. Bull and Dr. Oliver gave great support to the civil rights struggle in Spartanburg.

On the education side of the equation was Dr. Ellen C. Watson, a mentor/counselor to many students in Spartanburg. Dewey Tullis, who moved from Florida to Spartanburg after marrying a Spartanburg girl, Kitty Collins, worked in Greenville County during the day and in the evenings mentored young boys and worked at Collins Funeral Home. These educators would mentor and mold a cadre of disciples who would change Spartanburg forever. Many would affect the course of South Carolina for the foreseeable future.

C. Tyrone Gilmore was one of those disciples. Gilmore graduated from Carver High School and attended Livingstone College before returning home, where he rose to principal of his alma mater, Carver High. He later became the first black superintendent in the Spartanburg County school system as he headed School District 7.

James Talley, another graduate of Carver High, became one of the first blacks to serve on the Spartanburg City Council. In 1992, he was elected mayor of the city, becoming the first person of color to lead a large city in South Carolina. A former teacher and coach, he was not reelected as mayor. Some say the white business community wanted a different colored face in that office.

And then there were the disciples from the Toby Hartwell Projects. Donald W. Beatty was one of them. He was elected to the Spartanburg City Council in 1988, to the South Carolina House of Representatives in 1991, to the South Carolina Circuit Court in 1995 and to the South Carolina Court of Appeals in 2003. In 2007, he was elevated to the South Carolina Supreme Court.

The Grant brothers, Joe and Tony, came out of Toby Hartwell and made names for themselves. Joe, the elder of the two, attended Clemson, Wofford College and USC. There was a super militant streak in Joe. He became an advocate for justice in South Carolina. He headed the Minnesota Teachers Association for a period and then returned home to serve as executive director of the South Carolina Education Association for ten years. He became a registered lobbyist in the General Assembly. His little brother Tony played football at South Carolina State College and then pursued a career in banking. He and his wife, Helen, are founders of Grant Financial Services.

At the county council level, Johnny Code Stewart added color to that body and was later joined by Sallie Peake. Presently, Mike Brown holds a seat on the council. Sallie Peake is now the mayor of Wellford, a town in the county.

Hudson Barksdale Sr. became the first black to represent Spartanburg in the South Carolina House of Representatives. He was followed by Tee Ferguson, Donald Beatty, Brenda Lee (who served for ten years) and Harold Mitchell, who presently holds the seat.

Another disciple of Mrs. Ellen Watson was James Cheeks. A graduate of Wofford College, he practices law in the city and is a true advocate for the downtrodden.

The name Kevin Alexander Gray raises eyebrows when mentioned. In 1968, Gray integrated Fairforest Elementary School. In 1974, he led a student boycott at Dorman High School to protest a racial slur made by the school principal. He earned a bachelor's degree from Wofford College. He joined the U.S. Army and rose to the rank of captain. He returned home, and then Governor Dick Riley hired him to work in the CETA program. From 1984 to 1986, he was a producer and writer for *Conceptions*, a weekly fifty-five-minute news magazine for the new radio station in Columbia, WDPN, that was owned by Reverend I.D. Newman of NAACP fame. In 1987, Gray coordinated Jesse Jackson's campaign for president. After the campaign, he continued with Jackson's Rainbow/PUSH Coalition organization until 1990.

Finally, a Sumter native, Deloris Ham Oliver, who adopted Spartanburg after landing there to take a teaching position, married Dr. Eddie Oliver, the pharmacist. Ham was very active with the SCLC (Southern Christian Leadership Conference). She was immersed in the NAACP Youth Council activities in Sumter. She counts as friends national NAACP executive directors Walter White and Roy Wilkins and A. Phillip Randolph of the Sleeping Car Porters Union. These men sat at her parents' table in Sumter and plotted strategy for the civil rights movement.

For more details and coverage of black life in Spartanburg County, refer to *South of Main*, a publication compiled by Brenda Lee Pryce and Beatrice Hill. It covers the early years of Spartanburg from the 1900s to 1970.

THE SUMTER MOVEMENT

T alk to black senior citizens in Sumter, and they will tell you that their city has been the breeding ground for black leadership in South Carolina. Anchored by Morris College and Lincoln High School, the focus has always been on education. They will tell you about Johnson C. Whittaker, the second black person to attend West Point and later the principal of Lincoln High School. Whittaker was expelled from West Point because of some trumped-up charges. He was later exonerated. After his tenure at Lincoln, he taught at South Carolina State College, where his son, Miller F. Whittaker, who was born in Sumter, became the third president of that institution.

Black Sumterites will remind you that George Washington Murray, the last black person elected to Congress in 1892, was from Sumter. One hundred years later, his distant cousin, James E. Clyburn, would be the first black elected to Congress since Murray (more about Clyburn in a later chapter).

Over in Maysville, a rural town in the eastern part of Sumter County, is the site of the birthplace of Mary McLeod Bethune. While most of the country knew Mrs. Bethune for the founding of Bethune-Cookman College in Daytona Beach, Florida, her accomplishments were much greater. She was an advisor to President Franklin D. Roosevelt, and through her efforts, the first black general in the U.S. Army was nominated by Roosevelt in the person of Benjamin O. Davis Sr. in 1941. She was very close to the president's wife, Eleanor, and her request was transferred directly to the president. He acted swiftly in order to get Mrs. Roosevelt off his back. Mrs. Bethune was the founder of the National Council of Negro Women, and today a postage stamp honors her. Mrs. Bethune's last visit to Sumter was in April 1955. She came at the request of a young AME minister named Reverend Fred C. James and the mayor of Sumter, Priscilla Shaw. They organized a program to honor her at Mount Pisgah AME Church. Covering the event for the Lincoln High School *Echo* newspaper were James Gibson, Julius Capers, George Barno and James L. Felder. They had an opportunity to interview Mrs. McLeod. She died three weeks after that visit to Sumter and is buried on the campus of Bethune Cookman College.

At Lincoln High School, a dainty little lady name Agnes H. Wilson, who taught French and journalism and served as advisor to the *Echo* newspaper staff, took a delegation from the *Echo* to the Columbia University Scholastic Press Association annual meeting in New York City for over twelve years. The *Echo* won honors in its category for each of those years. One of those years, 1962, Mrs. Wilson allowed a non-Lincoln student the opportunity to take that trip. He was future astronaut Charles Bolden, who was a student at C.A. Johnson High School in Columbia. His mother, Mrs. Ethel Bolden, who knew Mrs. Wilson through Presbyterian Church circles, prevailed upon her to allow him to go. Mrs. Wilson, a graduate of Allen University, won Teacher of the Year in 1969 and was elected president of the South Carolina Education Association, a first for blacks in the state. During her tenure, the all-black PEA and the all-white SCTA merged under her leadership.

Dr. Agnes H. Wilson Burgess was the first black to serve as Teacher of the Year in South Carolina in 1969. She also presided over the merger of the black and white teachers' associations to form the SCEA.

In 1956, the safety patrol at Lincoln High School made history when it traveled to Washington, D.C., for the annual patrol outing. Other white schools from Sumter went on the trip as well. For the journey to D.C., the Lincoln students were seated in the "colored" coach and the white students in the "white coach." NAACP leaders in Sumter did not think it was fair, and they called ahead to Clarence Mitchell, the NAACP man in Washington, and alerted him to what was coming his way. Upon arrival in the nation's capital, the students were further segregated, as the black students, among whom were Francina Woods, Winifred Gadson, Clarence Taylor and James L. Felder, were housed in a "colored" fleabag hotel, while the white students were placed in an upscale Sheraton Hotel. Mitchell protested this arrangement, and the black students were moved to a better location. Upon returning to Sumter, word got out about what had happened in Washington. There were no more trips by the safety patrol to Washington during that era.

The turning point in civil rights in Sumter occurred in 1955. It was a year after *Brown v. Board*, and the school system was still rigidly segregated. The local NAACP officers circulated a petition for parents to sign seeking access for their children to attend white schools in Sumter School Districts 2 and 17. Retaliation by the white community began immediately. Pressure was put on some black parents to remove their names from the petition. When one black parent, Roland Blanding Sr., was confronted by Shep K. Nash, a local white attorney who represented the school board, Blanding indicated that he wanted his name removed from the petition. When word got back to the NAACP officers, they had a letter published in the *Sumter Daily Item* stating that somebody was lying about Blanding's signature and the petition. Nash sued the Sumter Branch NAACP and its officers. He sought $100,000 in damages. The parties he sued included Reverend H.P. Sharper, Dr. B.T. Williams, S.J. Robinson, Reverend J. Herbert Nelson, L.J. Peterson, J.J. Burrell, Reverend F.C. James, Reverend I. D. Newman, Dr. Edmond McDonald, Dr. E.C. Jones Sr., S.J. McDonald Sr., James Daniels and the Sumter Branch NAACP.

At this point in time, Sumter had no black lawyers. Matthew J. Perry, then of Spartanburg, and Lincoln C. Jenkins Jr. of Columbia would make their first foray into Sumter to represent these defendants. They lost at the local level and appealed to the South Carolina Supreme Court. They lost before this court, as well. The case was finally settled for $10,000, which was paid by a labor union.

Leroy F. Scott Sr., a black educator and supervisor of Negro elementary schools in Sumter County, was prophetic in 1954, when he mused about what to expect following the *Brown v. Board* decision. He said:

It appears that the major problem which confronts most of the states affected by the Supreme Court's decision is one of giving up an educational pattern which has been practiced for many generations. It is unwise and foolish for minority groups to expect an immediate reversal of present practices in the southern states, regardless of how right a thing may be. Perhaps a simple illustration at this point would be in order: Suppose you were driving a car at a high rate of speed and found it necessary to go in the opposite the direction. Would you stop the car, carefully turn around, and then proceed to your destination, or, would you suddenly put your car in reverse gear at a high rate of speed? What would you do?

Mr. Scott was right on target. It took another ten years following that decision before some measureable signs of desegregation could be seen.

In 1957, Reverend J. Herbert Nelson, a local Presbyterian minister and NAACP activist, was appointed by President Eisenhower to the South Carolina Advisory Commission of the U.S. Commission on Civil Rights. Then–lieutenant governor Ernest Hollings warned that anyone accepting an appointment of the commission would not be welcome in South Carolina. In later years, Hollings would moderate his stance on racial matters.

The KKK threatened Reverend Nelson and fired shots into his home in Sumter. His wife was threatened with being fired from her teaching position.

On March 4, 1960, a wave of students from Morris College and Lincoln High School hit the streets in Sumter and began sitting in at several drugstores and five-and-dime stores on Main Street. The student leaders in this movement included Morris College students William F. Randolph, Francis Dubose, Leroy Gary and Helen Richardson. The high school ringleader was Ralph W. Canty. The adults supporting the students were Reverend F.C. James, chair of the group; Willie Singleton Jr., treasurer of the group; Reverend D.D. Felder; Reverend J. Herbert Nelson; and Robert J. Palmer, who provided bail money. Again, Matthew J. Perry of Columbia was called in to defend the students. All of the students were found guilty at the local level, but on appeal, which took three years, they were exonerated. The fight for civil rights in Sumter was on its way.

In 1967, Sumter County got its first black elected official. Willie Jefferson, an Allen University graduate, won a seat on the Maysville Town Council. Later, James L. Solomon won a seat on the School District 17 Board of Trustees. In 1972, Ernest A. Finney Jr., after running four times for public office, won a seat in the South Carolina House of Representatives. Not to be forgotten is attorney Billy James, who ran for Sumter City Council in 1954.

Reverends F.C. James and A.W. Wright, leaders of the Sumter movement, check the list of names of jailed demonstrators to determine how much bail money must be raised. *Courtesy of Cecil Williams.*

The KKK burned a cross in his yard following his attempt to win a seat on the council.

A visit to Sumter County today reminds one of the Reconstruction era, when blacks held many public offices. Blacks holding elected positions include Anthony Dennis, sheriff; Carolina Richardson, treasurer; Lauretha McCants, auditor; and Ernest A. Finney III, solicitor. On the seven-member county council, there are four black members: Vivian Fleming-McGhaney, Eugene Baten, Naomi Sanders and Larry Blanding.

On the Sumter City Council, a six-member body, three are blacks: Iona Dwyer, Calvin Hastie and Thomas J. Lowery. Previously, the first blacks to serve on the city council were Willie Singleton Jr., Hattie Scarborough and Reverend William F. Randolph. The immediate past police chief and first black to serve in that position was Patty Patterson. On the legislative delegation in the South Carolina House of Representatives is David J. Weeks. He followed Ernest A. Finney Jr., Larry Blanding and Ralph Canty, all of whom served in the General Assembly.

In the area of education, Sumter County has been served by two school districts, 2 and 17. District 17 served the city residents, and District 2 served the rural areas of the county. Following the desegregation of schools in 1964, blacks have served as superintendents and board chairs in both districts. The first black to serve as superintendent in District 17 was Zona Jefferson, and two blacks, Jo R. White and Iona Dwyer, served as board chairs. In District 2, Naomi Sanders served as chair, and Joe Leftt was superintendent until his untimely death in an auto accident. Elijah McCants served the district during the 1980s, as well. Reverend Herbert Shackleford, a Presbyterian minister, was one of the early members of School District 17 board members. In 2011, the two school districts were combined into one Sumter County School District. Randolph Bynum is the new superintendent, and Larry Addison chairs the combined boards.

Not to be forgotten in law enforcement are those early pioneers who broke the color line at the sheriff's department. Lucius Felder and John B. Lewis were the first black deputies. On the city police force, C.E. Gillard, Charles Burns and Robert China were the first. They had limited authority, they could not arrest whites and their jurisdiction was limited to South Sumter.

Sumter once had a thriving black business district on Manning Avenue. Some referred to it as "Cross the Tracks." One could do most of his or her

Dr. Agnes H. Wilson Burgess, Congresswoman Shirley Chisholm and Jim Felder share a laugh at a reception for the congresswoman in Columbia in 1971.

shopping for clothing, food and medical supplies on the "Avenue." The need for going downtown was limited to banking and postal services or to attend the movies. In 1968, when the National Bank of South Carolina hired its first black tellers, Alicia Lewis, Elaine Jeter and Deanna Moore, they worked harder than the white tellers. It seemed that every black depositor would stand in one of the black teller lines and leave the other five white tellers with nothing to do but polish their nails. Blacks were proud to see these young ladies sitting in the teller cages.

For a small town, Sumter has its share of black funeral homes. There are eight, and five of them are on the same stretch of road.

Not to be overlooked is the Head Start program in Sumter. It was the first of its kind to be started in South Carolina and was spearheaded by Rubye J. Johnson. Mrs. Johnson is now retired, but the program and building are named in her honor.

In medicine, Sumter had its own black hospital. It was named Community Hospital and founded by Reverend H.B. Brown and the Job Society. There were always black physicians and dentists in Sumter, and they made house calls. The community never suffered from lack of medical care. Dr. W.F. Bultman became the chief of staff of Tuomey Hospital in 1977, a first for blacks in Sumter.

19

CLEMSON, USC, THE CITADEL AND WINTHROP INTEGRATE

C lemson removed its segregation barriers on January 26, 1963, when Harvey Gantt, a native of Charleston, was escorted to the campus by his attorney, Matthew J. Perry. Gantt had applied to Clemson for admission and was denied. He enrolled at the University of Iowa and challenged his denial in the courts. Following several appeals, he was admitted. A week before Gantt's enrollment, Governor Ernest F. Hollings addressed the General Assembly for his final time as governor. Hollings said, "If and when every legal remedy has been exhausted, this General Assembly must make clear South Carolina's choice, a government of laws rather than a government of men. We have run out of courts, and we have run out of time." This was the same Governor Hollings who had called the NAACP an illegal and subversive organization and had dared any black person to serve on the U.S. Civil Rights Commission Advisory Committee. Here he did a 180-degree turn for the betterment of South Carolina.

Gantt's transition at Clemson was uneventful. He finished Clemson's architectural program with honors. Today, he is an architect in Charlotte, North Carolina, where he has served on the city council and two terms as mayor of North Carolina's largest city. He ran a very close race for the U.S. Senate against Jesse Helms.

Clemson was the first white college in South Carolina to integrate. Nine months later, in September 1963, the University of South Carolina admitted three black students.

Harvey Gantt leaving the courtroom of the federal courthouse with his family after another day of fighting for admission to Clemson in 1960. *Courtesy of Cecil Williams.*

CLEMSON COLLEGE OPENED ITS DOORS in 1883 with 446 students and 51 faculty members. It was an all-male military college. In 1900, John Heisman, the individual for whom the Heisman Trophy is named, was Clemson's head football coach. He led the Tigers to an undefeated conference championship. In 1917, the entire senior class at Clemson enlisted in World War I. In 1955, the military system of discipline was dropped at Clemson, and women were allowed to enroll for the first time. In 1964, Clemson College was renamed and became Clemson University. There is one person of color on Clemson's board of trustees, Dr. Louis Lynn. Lynn is a 1970 graduate of the school. One of its first black faculty members was Dr. Dean Floyd, also a graduate of the class of 1970.

Clemson's football fans brag about their Tigers. They are quick to remind the USC fans that Clemson is the only South Carolina school to win a national football championship. The 1981 team beat Nebraska in the Orange Bowl to win that championship. Key players on that team included five black athletes. They were Terry Kinard, Perry Tuttle, Jeff Davis, William "the Refrigerator" Perry and Homer Jordan, the first black quarterback to play on a Clemson or USC team. As a result of the decision to allow Jordan to play, many blacks in the state began to favor Clemson over USC. Kinard, Davis and Tuttle were selected first-team all-Americans that year. Along with William Perry, they all had distinguished careers in the National Football League.

The University of South Carolina (USC) was founded in 1801 as an all-white college. It stayed that way until 1873, when blacks were accepted as students. The opening of USC to blacks occurred following the changes in the 1868 South Carolina Constitution, which provided that all educational institutions funded by the state would be "open to all the children and youths of the state" without regard to race and color. Implementation of this proposition began with the 1869 appointment of Francis L. Cardoza and Benjamin A. Bozeman to the USC Board of Trustees. Further implementation occurred with the admission of Henry E. Haynes in 1873 to the medical school. His admission was followed by the withdrawal of nearly all the white students and the medical school faculty from USC. Also in 1873, four blacks—Samuel J. Lee, J.A. Bowley, S.A. Swails and W.R. Gervay— were elected to the board of trustees, replacing Cardoza and Bozeman.

By 1877, the student body was 90 percent black. All of this black progress at the university ended with the 1876 presidential election, when a deal was cut to allow the federal troops to be withdrawn from the South, and the conservative Democrats took over the state again. Some of those outstanding graduates of the "Reconstruction University" included Francis L. Cardoza, who would serve as state treasurer, secretary of state and a delegate to the 1968 Constitutional Convention. Also, Richard T. Greener, the first black graduate of Harvard College and the USC Law School class of 1876, was a graduate. And there was Thomas E. Miller, who served in the U.S. Congress and became the first president of South Carolina State College in 1896.

USC REMAINED AN ALL-WHITE institution until the forced 1963 admission of Henri Monteith, Robert Anderson and James L. Solomon. However, blacks made numerous efforts from 1937 to 1960 to gain admission. In 1937, Charles Bruce Bailey, grandson of Parris Simkins, who graduated from USC Law School in 1876, sought and was denied admission to the law school.

In June 1946, John H. Wrighten III, a senior at South Carolina State College, applied to the law school and was denied because of this race. Wrighten sued USC and the board of trustees based on the principle of separate but equal, and as a result of his effort, the South Carolina General Assembly appropriated $60,000 for the establishment of a law school in Orangeburg.

From Peaceful Protests to Groundbreaking Rulings

In 1958, eleven black students from Allen University, who included Thelma McClain, Mary Hatton, James Jones, Cornell F. Mitchell and Loretta Jenkins, attempted to enroll at USC. They were denied admission. In 1960, Lloyd and Raymond Weston, two South Carolina State College students, applied for admission and were denied. In May 1962, Henri Monteith applied to USC and was denied. She went and enrolled at Notre Dame College in Maryland and filed suit against USC in October 1962 to gain entrance as a transfer student. USC admitted that Monteith was denied admission in May 1962 because of her race but that in her application for admission as a transfer student she had failed to include a transcript or submit to a physical exam.

While Monteith's lawsuit was pending, two other students applied: Robert Anderson seeking undergraduate admission and James L. Solomon Jr. seeking graduate school admission. On July 10, 1963, U.S. District Court judge J. Robert Martin ordered USC to admit the students beginning in the fall of 1963.

USC's board of trustees would remain lily white until the early 1980s, when Kay Patterson, a state representative from Columbia, would serve an eight-month period on the board. He was followed by Larry Weston of Sumter and Alberta Grimes of Greenville. Sam Foster Jr. of Rock Hill was elected by the General Assembly, replacing Weston and Grimes, and served until he was replaced by Leah Moody, a young lawyer from Rock Hill and the daughter of one of the state's outstanding athletes and coaches, Lindberg Moody, and Bessie Moody-Lawrence, a former member of the South Carolina House of Representatives.

USC hired its first black faculty member in 1968 in the person of Dr. Earline Cunningham in the Chemistry Department. Others joining her on the faculty were Tom Davis, James Luck, Sadie Logan, Roland Haynes Sr., Bobby Donaldson, Grace Jordan McFadden, Johnny McFadden, Cleveland Sellers, Andrew Chisholm and Gus Rogers. Over in the law school, O'Neal Smalls was the first black faculty member, and Ken Gaines joined him later. On January 8, 2004, the law school hired its first black dean, Burnelle Powell. The first female professor of law came in 2009 in the person of Daniel Holley-Walker.

At the staff level and in the president's office, Shirley Mills, a Sumter native and graduate of Columbia College, is director of government and community relations. Mills worked for Senator Ernest F. Hollings for ten years prior to joining USC. She brought a wealth of community experience to the president's office. Bobby Gist, a Union native and graduate of Benedict

College, serves as the director of equal opportunity. Prior to this assignment, he worked at the Human Affairs Commission and chaired the Columbia Housing Authority Board.

On campus in student affairs, Harry Walker became the first black Student Government Association president in 1972. His campaign manager was Luther Battiste. This student government election was Battiste's warm-up for his run for Columbia City Council in 1982. There have been eight or more blacks to serve as SGA president, including Steve Benjamin, who was elected mayor of Columbia in 2010. In 1974, USC elected its first black homecoming queen, Gail Denise Bush of Aiken.

On the sports staff at USC, Harold White was the first black coach to be hired in 1971, when he came aboard as a graduate assistant football coach. Upon his retirement thirty years later, he had served in many capacities. White witnessed the passing through USC of some outstanding athletes. There were Kevin Long and Clarence Williams, who in 1973 were the first players to rush for over one thousand yards in a single season. He saw George Rogers win the Heisman Trophy. He was there with Alex English and Casey Manning, two of the best basketball players to play hoops at USC. Manning was the first black player to play for Frank McGuire. After leaving the basketball court, Manning pursued a legal career and now serves on the judicial court.

In Charleston, The Citadel, the military college of South Carolina, lowered its barriers in 1965. Its first black student in the graduate program was Helen Richardson Rayon of Sumter. In 1966, the first black cadet was Charles Foster, and in 1967, the second black to enroll was Joseph Shine. After graduation and completing law school, he became counsel to the state Budget and Control Board. In 1994, after a strenuous legal battle, The Citadel admitted its first female, Shannon Faulkner.

Up in Rock Hill, Winthrop University, which at one time was the state-supported school for white women, admitted its first blacks in 1964. Winthrop became fully coed in 1974.

20

ADDING COLOR TO THE STATEHOUSE

Following the Civil War in 1864 and the passage of the Thirteenth, Fourteenth and Fifteenth Amendments, blacks began to use their political muscle and run for public office. South Carolina sent more black men to the U.S. Congress than any other southern state. In the South Carolina General Assembly, there were more blacks in the House of Representatives than whites. During this period, which is referred to as the Reconstruction era and which W.E.B. DuBois called the "mystic years," blacks controlled the chairmanships in the House. A northern reporter, James S. Pike, made a visit to the House of Representatives. He wrote the following: "The Speaker of the House is black. The chairman of the Ways & Means Committee is black. The chairman of the Judiciary Committee is black. The Sergeant-At-Arms is black and the Chaplain is 'coal black.'" This was enough to drive some white men mad, and in a sense it did.

The presidential election of 1876 would change South Carolina politically and socially in a drastic fashion. In that election between Rutherford B. Hayes, the Republican candidate from Ohio, and Samuel Tilden, the Democratic candidate from New York, Tilden won 51 percent of the popular vote to Hayes's 48 percent. However, Hayes won more votes in the Electoral College. The election was thrown into the U.S. House of Representatives. A deal was struck. The white Democrats from the South agreed to give Hayes their votes if he would agree to pull the federal troops out of the South and let them be about business as usual. The compromise was accepted, and the first act was to put in some black "codes" restricting the rights of black southerners and moving them into another kind of servitude. The South Carolina Constitution of 1895 all but eliminated any potential for blacks to be elected to public office. In that constitution, it legalized residency requirements, poll tax payments, literacy tests, a criminal background check and other incriminating items aimed specifically at blacks. By 1900, there were no blacks in the South Carolina General Assembly and a handful at the local level. There would be a seventy-year drought before blacks would again have a presence in the South Carolina Statehouse.

There were efforts as early as 1952 by blacks to run for the legislature, but no one was successful because there were not enough blacks registered in any county to elect a person of color. By 1970, five years after passage of the 1965 Voting Rights Act, over 200,000 blacks were placed on the voter rolls in South Carolina after a successful voter registration campaign coordinated by the NAACP and the South Carolina Voter Education Project (VEP). It was now felt in some quarters, and by many, that it was time to make a serious run for seats in the South Carolina General Assembly. Eight black candidates ran for the House of Representatives in the 1970 Democratic Party primary. In Charleston, Jim Clyburn, Herbert Fielding and George Payton ran. In Columbia, it was Jim Felder and I.S. Leevy Johnson. Jesse Lawrence ran in Williamsburg County, Highland Davis in Beaufort County and Reverend C.M. Johnson in Spartanburg County. There was no such thing as a single-member district in 1970. All candidates ran countywide, and the top vote getters won the seats. South Carolina had in place at the time a plan called "full slate voting." It meant that in Richland County, for example, voters were required to vote for the total number of seats that were available or the vote would be voided or thrown out. It further meant that one had to vote for candidates he did not know or did not want to vote for in order to have his vote counted.

In order to get elected during these times, some deals had to be made. In 1970, Richland County was entitled to ten seats in the House of Representatives, and there were nine incumbents running. I.S. Leevy Johnson and Jim Felder wanted two of those seats. This meant that one of the incumbents had to bite the dust. Lewis J. Cromer, chairman of the Richland County Democratic Party, took a lot of heat when he proposed that Johnson and Felder be given support by the white Democrats to ensure victory for them. It happened, and the two of them were elected. Down in Charleston, a similar situation occurred in which Clyburn and Fielding were seeking two of eleven House seats. It worked 100 percent for them in the June primary but only 50 percent in the November general election. Clyburn went to bed a winner in the November general election and woke up to find that he had lost because of absentee ballots and error in transposing the numbers. Fielding did win. None of the other black candidates won that

Jim Felder and I.S. Leevy Johnson after being sworn into the South Carolina House of Representatives in 1971. Along with Herbert Fielding, they were the first blacks to be elected since Reconstruction.

year. South Carolina saw its first three black faces take seats in the House of Representatives since Reconstruction.

In Columbia, a lot of credit goes to some young white political aspirants (in addition to Lewis Cromer), who called themselves the "Young Turks." They included Isadore Lourie, Travis Medlock, Alex Sanders, Robert Kneece and Kirkman Finlay Jr., who would later become mayor of Columbia.

Upon arriving in Columbia in January 1971, Herbert Fielding's first act was to introduce a bill, supported by Jim Felder and I.S. Leevy Johnson, to do away with full-slate countywide voting and the establishment of single-member districts. The Speaker of the House, Solomon Blatt, appointed Jim Felder to serve on the committee to draw these districts. This committee, composed of House and senate members, was chaired by Senator Marion Gressette of Calhoun County. It dragged its feet, and nothing materialized. In 1974, a lawsuit was filed under the 1965 Voting Rights Act that forced the General Assembly to draw lines for individual House districts.

By 1975, thirteen blacks had been elected to the House, and the Legislative Black Caucus was organized and chaired by Ernest A. Finney Jr. of Sumter.

Initially, the caucus won some symbolic victories. There was the passing of legislation that authorized the portrait of Mary McLeod Bethune to be hung in the state capitol building. The caucus had to fight to make Dr. Martin Luther King's birthday a state holiday. Later, it would push for the passage of a procurement statue that required consideration of minority businesses in state contracts. A governor's office for small and minority business was created, and the Human Affairs Commission was given state agency status. Otherwise, the caucus prevented some bad legislation from becoming law by simply being there.

From 1970 to 1983, blacks only held seats in the House of Representatives. There was no one in the senate. That would end in a special election held on October 25, 1983, when Reverend I.D. Newman, an icon of the civil rights movement, having spent thirty years on the front line with the NAACP, won that election and became the first black senator to serve since Reconstruction. Reverend Newman resigned from the senate in 1985 for health reasons and was replaced by House member Kay Patterson, who served until 2008, when he retired.

By 1984, the black caucus members had increased to twenty-five, and they were beginning to grow independent of from the white Democrats and started a push for more single-member districts. The caucus played a major

Reverend I.D. Newman is sworn in as the first black state senator since Reconstruction in 1984. *Courtesy of Cecil Williams.*

and controversial role in the legislative reapportionment fight. Sometimes there were temporary political alliances of convenience with Republicans. The November 1984 election boosted the caucus numbers to thirty, mainly as a result of drawing new district lines to maximize the number of blacks who could be elected. The same redrawing of lines created more almost completely white districts. This helped Republicans gain a majority in the House for the first time since Reconstruction. However, this time it was a Republican-controlled House by whites.

In the 2000 legislative session, the Confederate flag surfaced as a very important issue facing the people of South Carolina. The NAACP organized a march and rally at the capitol that included over fifty thousand participants. It prodded the legislature to do something. All caucus members were not on the same page about what to do with the flag, but they all agreed that it needed to come off the dome and out of the House and senate chambers. It was removed from those three places and placed at the Confederate Monument, which stands in front of the north side of the capitol. The NAACP has placed sanctions against the state for having it there. The state has lost many conventions and meetings as a result of where the flag is today. It continues to be a divisive issue.

In the 2008 election cycle, the caucus would see the first black Republican elected to the statehouse since Reconstruction in the person of Tim Scott of Charleston. Scott won a seat in the North Charleston area. He had served for thirteen years on the Charleston County Council prior to this race. Later, Scott would win a seat in the U.S. Congress as a Republican from the First Congressional District.

In 1982, Mary Miles of Calhoun County won the House District 93 seat, which was held by John Gressette Felder, the nephew of Senator Marion Gressette. It was one of South Carolina's biggest upsets in recent history. Miles refused to join the caucus. Some say she felt that she did not receive enough support from caucus members in her run for the House, and she kept her distance.

The Speaker of the House appoints all standing committee chairs. Since the inception of the caucus, only one committee has had a black chair: the Medical, Municipal and Military Affairs (MMM) Committee. Juanita White of Jasper County was the first chair of that committee, followed by Joe E. Brown of Columbia and Leon Howard of Columbia.

In addition to the current twenty-eight House members and nine senators, there have been forty-six other blacks who served in the House and senate since 1970.

The caucus has been served by six executive directors. The first was Dr. Jimmy Gilbert, who later was elevated to a presiding elder in the AME Zion Church; he was also owner of a State Farm Insurance Agency. Dalton Trezevant followed Gilbert and moved on to Congressman Jim Clyburn's staff. Walker E. Solomon Jr. was the third, and he moved on to head the Department of Social Services Office in Florence. Shirley Robinson, the fourth director, is now an administrative law judge for the state. Gwen Bynoe, the fifth director, is the executive liaison to the General Assembly for the South Carolina Retirement System. The current director is Juanzena Johnson. It seems that a stint at the black caucus office can lead to other rewarding opportunities.

Finally, on a visit to the statehouse today, one will see portraits of black South Carolina natives displayed in the House and senate chambers and the lobby. A portrait of Dr. Benjamin E. Mays, native of Greenwood and longtime president of Morehouse College, hangs in the House chambers. Reverend I.D. Newman's portrait hangs in the senate chambers. A beautiful portrait of Mary McLeod Bethune graces the lobby of the capitol. The portraits of two blacks who served as lieutenant governors, R.H. Cleaves and A.J. Ransier, are in the Lieutenant Governor's Office. Two blacks who served as Speaker of the House, Samuel Lee and Robert B. Elliott, both of Aiken, are displayed in the House chamber. On April 25, 1995, Modjeska Monteith Sinkins's portrait was unveiled at the statehouse. A committee

Dr. Benjamin E. Mays, a Greenwood County native and president of Morehouse College. His portrait hangs in the statehouse.

headed by Representative Alma Bird and Senator Kay Patterson organized the event. In my capacity as executive director of the NAACP at that time, I delivered a tribute to Mrs. Simkins on that occasion.

REMEMBERING MODJESKA

A Tribute to Mary Modjeska Monteith Simkins

It is only fitting and proper that a portrait of Mary Modjeska Monteith Simkins be unveiled here today in this statehouse in remembrance of her. I remember Modjeska for being one of the founding members of the South Carolina Conference of Branches NAACP.

I remember Modjeska for serving as the first field secretary of the South Carolina NAACP and receiving no pay for her work.

I remember Modjeska for discovering that white teachers were earning more than black teachers in 1943, and she pushed for litigation that led to Thompson v. Gibbes *and the equalization of teachers' pay in South Carolina in 1945.*

I remember Modjeska giving civil rights seminars to students from Allen University and Benedict College from behind the teller cage at Victory Savings Bank on Harden Street.

I remember Modjeska, who would drive alone to Clarendon County for a mass meeting and then would have the last word in the debate after the meeting in Billy Fleming's house at his bar.

I remember Modjeska, who cranked out more press releases and letters to the editor than all of the civil rights groups in South Carolina combined.

I remember Modjeska, who had a great sense of humor and was quite a crowd pleaser, but she was a fierce warrior for preserving freedom for all of us.

I remember Modjeska, who was just as at ease registering winos to vote on Read Street as she was entertaining Thurgood Marshall at her home on Marion Street.

A and I will remember Modjeska as a legend in her own time. She was our Harriett Tubman and our Sojourner Truth. She was a woman who woke up every morning with freedom on her mind.

So after today, when you happen to be passing the statehouse one evening and the lights are flashing and the building is shaking, do not be alarmed, for that will just be Modjeska debating with Edgar Brown, Sol Blatt, Marion Gressette and Ben Tillman, and she will be winning the argument.

PREVIOUS CAUCUS CHAIRPERSONS

Rep. Ernest Finney Jr., 1973–74
Rep. Theo W. Mitchell, 1974–75
Rep. I.S. Leevy Johnson 1976–77
Rep. Robert R. Woods, 1977–79
Rep. McKinley Washington, 1979–81
Sen. John Matthews Jr., 1981–84
Rep. Larry Blanding, 1984–87
Rep. Juanita White, 1987–89
Sen. Kay Patterson, 1989–90
Sen. Herbert U. Fielding, 1990–92

Rep. Joe E. Brown, 1992–94
Sen. Maggie Glover, 1994–96
Rep. John L. Scott Jr., 1996–98
Sen. John Matthews Jr., 1998–2000
Rep. Joseph H. Neal, 2000–02
Rep. Jerry N. Govan Jr., 2002–04
Rep. David J. Mack III, 2004–06
Rep. Leon Howard, 2006–08
Rep. J. David Weeks, 2008–10

PREVIOUS CAUCUS MEMBERS

Representatives

Kenneth Bailey, Orangeburg, 1985–92
Hudson Barksdale (d. 1986), Spartanburg, 1975–81
Donald W. Beatty, Spartanburg, 1990–95
Larry Blanding, Sumter, 1977–91
Floyd Breeland, Charleston, 1992–2008
Thomas D. Broadwater, Richland, 1981–84
Joe E. Brown, Richland, 1986–2006
Theodore Brown, Georgetown-Williamsburg-Horry, 1994–2000
Alma Byrd, Richland, 1991–98
Ralph Canty, Sumter, 1991–2000
Wilbur L. Cave, Allendale-Barnwell-Bamberg, 1994–98
James Faber, Richland, 1984–91
Ennis Fant, Greenville, 1989–91
James Felder, Columbia, 1971–72
Tee Ferguson (d. 2011), Spartanburg, 1983–90
Ernest A. Finney Jr., Sumter, 1972–75
Samuel Foster, York, 1981–92
Tobias Gadson Sr. (d. 1984), Charleston, 1981–84
Juanita Goggins (d. 2010), York, 1974–78
Benjamin. J. Gordon (d. 1997), Williamsburg-Berkeley, 1973–91
Amos L. Gourdine, Berkeley, 1996–2004

Anton Gunn, Richland, 2008–10
Cathy Harvin (d. 2010), Clarendon, 2008–10
Jesse E. Hines, Florence-Darlington, 1992–2006
Mack T. Hines, Florence-Marion, 1995–2006
Curtis Inabinett, Charleston-Colleton, 1991–2000
Isaac C. Joe, Lee-Sumter, 1981–84
I.S. Leevy Johnson, Richland, 1971–72; 1975–82
Kenneth Kennedy, Williamsburg, 1991–2010
Brenda Lee, Spartanburg, 1995–2005
Walter Lloyd (d. 2005), Colleton-Beaufort, 1994–2005
Daniel Martin, Charleston, 1985–92
Frank McBride, Richland, 1984–91
Willie B. McMahand, Greenville, 1992–98
Earl Middleton (d. 2007), Orangeburg, 1975–84
Mary P. Miles, Calhoun-Orangeburg-Lexington, 1982–84
Herbert L. Mitchell, Orangeburg, 1984–86
Bessie Moody-Lawrence, York, 1992–2008
Joseph R. Murray, Charleston, 1975–82
Julius Murray, Richland, 1979–84
Timothy Scott, Charleston, 2008–10
Sara V. Shelton (d. 1994), Greenville, 1984–88
Levola Taylor, Richland, 1991–92
Luther Taylor (d. 1997), Richland, 1983–90
Lucille Whipper, Charleston, 1986–96
Juanita White (d. 2011), Jasper-Beaufort, 1980–96
Robert R. Woods, Charleston, 1973–86

Senators

Herbert Fielding, Charleston, 1985–92 (House, 1971–73; 1983–84)
Frank Gilbert (d. 1999), Florence-Darlington, 1989–92 (House, 1983–88)
Maggie Glover, Florence-Darlington, 1992–2004 (House, 1989–92)
Theo Mitchell, Greenville, 1985–95 (House, 1975–84)
I. DeQuincey Newman (d. 1985), Chester-Fairfield-Richland (House, 1983–85)
Kay Patterson, Richland, 1985–2008 (House, 1975–85)
McKinley Washington, Charleston-Colleton, 1991–2000 (House, 1975–1990)
Dewitt Williams, Berkeley-Charleston-Colleton-Dorchester-Georgetown, 1996–97 (House, 1983–96)

CURRENT CAUCUS MEMBERS

Officers

Rep. William "Bill" Clyburn, Chairman
Rep. Harold Mitchell, Chairman Elect
Rep. J. David Weeks, Immediate Past Chairman
Rep. John R. King, Secretary
Rep. Chandra Dillard, Treasurer
Rep. Terry Alexander, Chaplain
Rep. Ronnie A. Sabb, Parliamentarian
Sen. John W. Matthews, Chairman Designee

Senators

Ralph Anderson
Robert Ford
Darrell Jackson
Gerald Malloy

Floyd Nicholson
Clementa C. Pinckney
John L. Scott
Kent Williams

Representatives

Karl B. Allen
Carl L. Anderson
Curtis Brantley
Robert L. Brown
Gilda Cobb-Hunter
Mia Butler Garrick
Wendell Gilliard
Jerry N. Govan
Christopher Hart
Kenneth Hodges
Lonnie Hosey

Leon Howard
Joseph H. Jefferson
Kevin L. Johnson
David J. Mack
Joseph McEachern
Joseph H. Neal
J. Anne Parks
J. Todd Rutherford
Bakari Sellers
J. Seth Whipper
Robert Williams

*Lists adapted from the South Carolina Legislative Black Caucus website, http://www.sclbc.org.

21

TAKING SEATS ON THE BENCH

In 1870, the South Carolina General Assembly elected its first black to the bench of the state Supreme Court in the person of Jonathan J. Wright. He served from 1870 to 1876. Wright came to Beaufort in 1865 to teach newly freed slaves about their legal rights. In the first election in which freed men could vote, in 1868, Wright was elected to the South Carolina Senate. A year later, he was elected to the Supreme Court. When the state's old white power regained control of the legislature in 1876, he was pushed off the court based on some trumped-up charges. He went to Charleston, where he practiced law and started a law school at Claflin College. In 1885, he died of tuberculosis at age forty-five.

Thanks to Richard and Belinda Gergel, who found a picture of Jonathan J. Wright in a rare bookstore while visiting New York City, people in South Carolina now can see an image of him. Richard Gergel met with members of the South Carolina Supreme Court in 1997, and a decision was made to commission the painting of a portrait of Wright from the print found by the Gergels and hang it in the Supreme Court's building. Chief Justice Ernest A. Finney had been searching for years for a picture of Wright. The Gergels are white. Richard was appointed by President Barack Obama to a U.S. District Court judgeship for South Carolina in 2011. Belinda is a member of the Columbia City Council and a retired professor from Columbia College.

It would be another one hundred years before the General Assembly would elect another black to the South Carolina judicial system. In 1976, Ernest A. Finney Jr. of Sumter was elected to the circuit court. In South Carolina, the road to a seat on the bench runs through the legislature.

That changed some in the 1980s. Prior to the 1980s, most judges who were elected came from the legislature or were former legislators. The members of the House and senate took care of their own. Finney followed that path. After running four times for public office in Sumter, he was elected to the House in 1972. Finney was called the black fox of the legislature. It was not meant to be demeaning, but it was because of his cleverness in working the levers of power in the statehouse to get things done. He knew which buttons to push, and he got to know the Speaker of the House, Solomon Baltt of Barnwell County, close up. He traveled often to Barnwell to enjoy bourbon and branch water with the old man. In 1985, Finney was elevated to the South Carolina Supreme Court, and nine years later he was named chief justice of the court. He served until his retirement in 2000.

There are six tiers in the South Carolina court system. There is the Supreme Court, the court of appeals, the circuit court, the family court, the administrative law judge court and the magistrates' court. The legislature elects the judges for all of these courts except the magistrates' court. In the old days, all one had to do was get to know the legislators, spend some time at the statehouse lobbying them and secure enough pledges to get elected. The election was done in a joint session of the senate and House, and one needed 85 of the 170 votes of this body to win a seat on the bench. The system has changed some in recent years; now one must be screened by a merit selection panel, which is composed of legislators and laymen, before his or her name is submitted to the General Assembly for a vote.

Magistrates' court judges are selected differently from those of the other courts. In the old days, prior to the 1980s, to become a magistrate one had to run in the June Democratic primary and win a judgeship. Qualifications did not mean very much. One did not have to be a high school graduate to qualify. All that counted was winning the primary, and thus you became a magistrate judge. As the Republicans became more of a force in South Carolina, they cried foul on the process, indicating that it was unfair to have one party controlling a big division of the judicial system. The process was changed, and now in order to become a magistrate, the local senator must nominate to the governor a candidate for approval by the senate. There are over 280 magistrates in South Carolina, and they carry the bulk load of criminal and civil cases. There are limitations on their jurisdiction, however. They cannot try felony cases or handle any family court matters. However, it is the magistrate that most individuals will encounter in the judicial system at some time in their lives, be it in the form of a traffic violation, a bad check, simple assault, eviction of a tenant, a preliminary hearing or suing for a small claim.

The first black magistrate in South Carolina was Joseph Stroy of Hopkins, in Richland County, in 1966. He won the Democratic primary and was sworn in. In Beaufort County that same year, Anthony Eddings and Eddie Kline were elected magistrates. In 1970, Jesse F. Stephens and Hattie Sims of Richland County joined the magistrate court system. They were followed by Walter Jones, for whom the Richland County Central Court is named; Franchot A. Brown; Sam Peay; Goldie Augustus; Mildred McDuffie; and Glenn Davis, all of Richland County. Over in Sumter, George Gibson and Daisey Moore took seats on the magistrate court. In Dorchester County, Vickie DeLee, daughter of civil rights icon Victoria DeLee, became a magistrate in 1978. Others would be selected in other parts of the state.

There are local courts in every town and city. In these municipalities, the city or town council hires on a contractual basis a judge to run these courts. The first black municipal court judge in South Carolina was Richard Fields of Charleston. He was selected in 1967 and later was elected to the family court and then to the circuit court in 1982. Today, at age ninety-one, he is very active and goes to his law office every day. Arthur McFarland followed Fields on the Charleston Municipal bench and rose to chief judge of that court.

Up the coast from Charleston in Myrtle Beach, the chief municipal judge is Jennifer Wilson. This Spellman College and Rutgers Law School graduate is married to the first black solicitor in South Carolina, Ralph Wilson.

In the Columbia Municipal Court, there has been a father-and-son presence. Lincoln C. Jenkins Jr. and Lincoln C. Jenkins III have served as chief judges in that court.

The South Carolina Supreme Court is a five-member bench. Today, in 2011, Donald Beatty serves on that court, keeping a black presence there since Chief Justice Finney retired. Beatty followed the same path that Finney did to reach the Supreme Court. He served in the House of Representatives. He was elected to the circuit court and the court of appeals and then to the Supreme Court. In the history of South Carolina, three persons of color have served on the Supreme Court: Jonathan J. Wright, Ernest A. Finney Jr. and Donald Beatty.

The South Carolina Court of Appeals is a nine-member bench. Its first black member was Jasper M. Cureton of Columbia, who was elected in 1985. He was followed by Donald W. Beatty of Spartanburg, and today the lone black member on this court is John D. Geathers of Columbia.

The South Carolina Circuit Court is a forty-five-member bench. Past black members on this court, in addition to Finney, include Richard Fields and Danny Martin of Charleston, Joseph Wilson and Reggie Lloyd of Columbia and the late Tee Ferguson of Spartanburg. Current black members include Deadra L. Jefferson of Charleston and, from Columbia, Casey L. Manning, Clifton Newman, Allison Lee and Deadra G. Benjamin. While Columbia is home to many of these judges, they are assigned to hear cases all over the state. Presently, there are only five black circuit court judges out of forty-five on this bench. There is concern among black legislators and the black community in general that there are not more judges of color on this bench.

The South Carolina Family Court bench has fifty-one seats. The earlier black members on this court, in addition to Richard Fields, included Harold Boulware of Columbia, Willie T. Smith of Greenville, Ruben Gray of Sumter and Abigail Rogers, Joe Wilson and Jasper M. Cureton, all of Columbia. Current members on this court include Angela R. Taylor of Sumter, Qwendolyn Y. Smalls of Columbia, Daniel E. Martin Jr of Charleston, Robert N. Jenkins and Alex Kinlaw Jr. of Greenville and Jan B. Holmes of Georgetown. Again, the concern is that there are only six blacks on a bench of fifty-one seats on a court that has a caseload of over 50 percent black juveniles.

There are forty-six probate courts, one representing each county. The probate judge is an elected position. There is only one black probate judge in South Carolina in Williamsburg County, and her name is Rudell M. Gambell. Early probate judges were Bernard Fielding of Charleston, who first served as an associate judge and later was elected to two terms at that position, and Harry C. Brown of Jasper County.

The master-in-equity judge is an appointed position. This court handles real estate foreclosures and other matters referred to it by the circuit court. Jasper M. Cureton was the first black to hold this position in Richland County. He was followed by Joseph M. Strickland, who is presently serving.

The final court in the state judicial system is the South Carolina Administrative Law Judge Court. This is a relatively new, six-bench court. One person of color sits on this court: Shirley Robinson.

In 2005, when no black candidates for judgeships were elected by the General Assembly, members of the black caucus staged a walkout in protest of the unfairness of that action. The next time around, some blacks were elected to judgeships.

Becoming a federal judge is a whole different ball of wax compared to the state process of selecting judges. In order to sit on the federal bench, one has to be recommended by his or her U.S. senator and/or congressman to the president of the United States, who then nominates that person to the U.S. Senate for confirmation after proper vetting. The first person of

Judge Matthew J. Perry served as general counsel for the state and national NAACP. In 1975, he was appointed to the United States Court of Military Appeals by President Gerald Ford, becoming the first black federal judge in the South. In 1977, President Jimmy Carter appointed him to the United States District Court, a lifetime appointment. He served until his death in 2011.

color to go through this process from South Carolina—and the South, for that matter—was Matthew J. Perry of Columbia. Perry, the master civil rights lawyer in South Carolina, was recommended to President Gerald Ford by Senator Strom Thurmond in 1975 for a seat on the U.S. Military Court of Appeals. This court had only a fifteen-year term of service. President Jimmy Carter, in 1979, nominated Perry for a lifetime appointment to the U.S. District Court for South Carolina. Perry served on the court until his death in 2011. The federal courthouse, located at 901 Richland Street in Columbia, is named the Matthew J. Perry Jr. Federal Courthouse in honor of Perry. On Friday, April 3, 2004, the dedication ceremony took place at 2:30 p.m. Judges, lawyers and everyday citizens filled the courtyard to witness that event.

Today, there are nine active U.S. District Court judges in South Carolina. Two are black females, Margaret B. Seymour of Columbia and J. Michelle Childs of Greenville. The federal court system has a magistrates' court level. Magistrates are elected by the U.S. district judges for an eight-year term. There is one black female magistrate, Jacquelyn Graham Austin, currently serving.

Two of the supporting units of the federal court system are the U.S. Marshal Service and the U.S. Probation Office. The U.S. marshal is appointed by the president. President Jimmy Carter appointed the first black U.S. marshal when Andrew Chisholm was named in 1977. President Clinton appointed

I.S. Leevy Johnson is surrounded by Judge Matthew J. Perry, Judge Jasper M. Cureton, Judge Lincoln C. Jenkins Jr. and Justice E.A. Finney as they congratulate him on being elected the first black president of the South Carolina Bar Association.

Israel Brooks, and the current marshal, Kelvin Washington, was named by President Obama in 2011.

The U.S. Probation Office is headed by Dickie Brunson, a native of Sumter and a graduate of Claflin University, the first black to hold this position. Brunson, the chief probation officer, was selected by all the federal judges sitting in South Carolina. On Sunday mornings, he can be found serving as superintendent of church school at the Union Station AME Church in Sumter. On the third Sunday of each month, he is on the choir, singing along with another fellow U.S. probation officer, Bryan Sowell.

The first person to add color to the U.S. Probation Office was Sam Goodwin. Goodwin, a Benedict College graduate, served as a warden in the South Carolina Correction System prior to his move to the U.S. Probation Office.

In order to take a seat on the bench, one must be a lawyer and a member of the South Carolina Bar Association. In 1960, Ernest A. Finney Jr., who later became chief justice of the South Carolina Supreme Court, could not join the South Carolina Bar Association. In 1994, I.S. Leevy Johnson of Columbia was elected the first black president of the state bar association. He was followed by Carl Solomon, the son of James L. Solomon Jr., in 2010.

22

JIM CLYBURN GOES TO WASHINGTON

In the spring of 1953, two Sumter youths, James E. Clyburn, age thirteen, and James L. Felder, age fourteen, joined the Sumter NAACP Youth Council. The council was housed at Mount Pisgah AME Church, and a young minister named Reverend Fred C. James was shepherd of the flock. Ms. Mitt Pringle was the advisor. At that meeting, Clyburn was elected president and Felder vice-president of the council. This would be the beginning of the political careers for both of them. For the next forty years, their lives would intersect and run parallel in many ways. First, they were both sons of beauticians, Almeta Dizzley Clyburn and Lillian Felder Golden. The two Jameses were leaders in the civil rights movement of 1960, Clyburn at South Carolina State College and Felder at Clark College in Atlanta. Both pledged Omega Psi Phi fraternity. Both married librarians. Clyburn married his college sweetheart, Emily England of Moncks Corner, and Felder married his high school sweetheart, Charletta Pickering of Sumter. Their wives worked together as librarians at the VA Hospital in Columbia for over thirty years. They lived in the Greenview neighborhood for over twenty years, the Clyburns on Juniper Street and the Felders on Easter Street. Their children attended Greenview Elementary School and Keenan High School. They ran for the South Carolina House of Representatives at the same time in 1970, Clyburn in Charleston and Felder in Columbia. Both won the Democratic primary in June, but Clyburn came up short in the November general election. Both served on the board of trustees of Penn Center on St. Helena Island. They both spent time on Capitol Hill in Washington, D.C. Felder served as a special assistant to Congressman John

Conyers of Michigan from 1965 to 1967. Clyburn made it to Capitol Hill in 1993 as the congressman from the Sixth Congressional District of South Carolina and continues to serve in 2011.

Clyburn's lost bid for the South Carolina House of Representatives in 1970 was a blessing in that another door opened when Governor John C. West offered him a position in the Governor's Office, where no blacks had served since Reconstruction. West hired two other persons of color, Margaret Purcell and George Hamilton of Walterboro. These three were placed in an office in the southeast corner of the Governor's Office. It was given the name "Ebony Suite."

Governor West created a division called Human Affairs and appointed Hamilton to head that office. In 1974, that division gained agency status, and West assigned Clyburn to head it as commissioner.

At the Human Affairs Commission, Clyburn fought to expand the jurisdiction of the agency to include public and private matters of discrimination in employment. He successfully secured the South Carolina Bill of Rights for handicapped citizens. In 1990, he convinced the General Assembly to approve only the second in the nation Fair Housing law. He built a strong agency at Human Affairs, but the politics of serving in public office was still in his blood.

In 1978, he ran for secretary of state. In a three-way race that included John Campbell, former mayor of Columbia, and Representative Mike Jolly of Gaffney, he lost his bid. He ran a second time for secretary of state in 1986 and lost. However, that race was the warm-up for his 1992 congressional bid.

In 1992, as a result of reapportionment and federal court action, a majority/minority congressional district was created in South Carolina and centered on the Florence area. There were five black candidates in the August Democratic primary that year. They included Senator Frank Gilbert of Florence; Ken Moseley, a professor at South Carolina State College; John Roy Harper, NAACP general counsel; Senator Herbert Fielding of Charleston; and Jim Clyburn, Human Affairs commissioner. Clyburn won the primary with 56 percent of the vote. Following the election, there was some bitterness expressed by some of the candidates, and one of them predicted Clyburn would not win the general election over a white Republican. His opponent in the general election was Florence city councilman John Chase. Clyburn beat him three to one in that election. Off to Washington, D.C., Jim Clyburn went.

Clyburn reported to the U.S. Congress in 1993 as the first black congressman from South Carolina since his distant cousin, George Washington Murray,

From Peaceful Protests to Groundbreaking Rulings

James E. "Jim" Clyburn was the first black congressman to serve in the U.S. Congress since Reconstruction. He followed in the footsteps of his distant cousin, George Washington Murray, who was the last person of color to serve from South Carolina in 1893. Both of them are Sumter natives.

served in 1893. He hit the ground running. He was elected co-president of his freshman class and quickly rose to a leadership rank. He was elected chairman of the congressional Black Caucus in 1999, and his reputation as a consensus builder helped him win a three-way race for chair of the House Democratic Caucus. When Democrats regained the House majority in 2006, Clyburn was elected by his colleagues to House whip, the third-highest position in the U.S. House of Representatives.

As a national leader, he has worked to respond to the needs of America's diverse communities. He championed community development of rural water projects, community health centers and broad-band connections. He has supported higher education by leading the charge for increasing Pell Grants, investing millions in science and math programs and funding for historic preservation at HBCUs. He has encouraged economic development by securing funding for empowerment zones, investing in green technology and directing 10 percent of recovery act funding to communities that have been 20 percent under the poverty level for the past thirty years.

As one who is sensitive to history, he has been able to lift up and recognize ancestors who have gone unknown. One example is Johnson C. Whittaker.

Whittaker was the second black person to attend West Point and was expelled after having been severely beaten by other cadets. West Point officials claimed the wounds were self-inflicted and wouldn't grant him his commission. In March 1994, along with Congressman John Spratt, Clyburn was able to attach an amendment to the Defense Department budget that authorized President Clinton to grant a posthumous officer's commission to this Camden, South Carolina native. Senator Ernest F. Hollings supported it on the Senate side, and the bill passed in May 1994.

Another masterful stroke of preserving the legacy of our elders was a bill Clyburn introduced in his first year to authorize the construction of the new federal courthouse in Columbia and name it the Matthew J. Perry Federal Courthouse. This was something rare for a freshman congressman to pursue. There were many forces opposed to the naming, including the Strom Thurmond crowd. They thought it should have been named for the senator, but Clyburn prevailed.

Jim Clyburn has become the most powerful congressman from South Carolina in recent years. President Obama has said, "He is one of a handful of people who, when they speak, the entire Congress listens."

As a result of his work and delivery of services, many buildings, awards and events have been named for him in South Carolina:

The Clyburn Fish Fry, Columbia
James E. Clyburn Aero Space Education Lab, Columbia
James E. Clyburn Community Center, Charleston
James E. Clyburn Community Empowerment Center, Orangeburg
James E. Clyburn Connector (a proposed bridge over Lake Marion)
James E. Clyburn Endowment Fund at South Carolina State University
James E. Clyburn Golf Center, Columbia
James E. Clyburn Health Center, Columbia
James E. Clyburn Intermodal Transportation Center, Sumter
James E. Clyburn Pedestrian Overpass (over Highway 277), Columbia
James E. Clyburn Research Center–MUSC, Charleston
James E. Clyburn Scholarship and Research Foundation, Columbia
James E. Clyburn Technology Center, Columbia
James E. Clyburn Transportation Research and Conference Center, Orangeburg
Jim Clyburn/Rudolph Canzatar Golf Classic Tournament, Santee

With sixteen buildings, monuments and events named for him, only the late Senator Thurmond has more, with seventeen. Since Clyburn has not announced that he plans to retire any time soon, more building and events may be in the making.

On the family side, Jim Clyburn's oldest daughter, Mignon, was nominated by President Obama on June 25, 2009, for a seat on the Federal Communications Commission. This is the agency that regulates TV, radio, cable and all other forms of communication in the country. His second daughter, Jennifer, is married to Walter Reed, and the third, Angela, is married to Cecil Hannibal. There are three grandchildren: Walter, Sidnye and Laila. Jim has two brothers, John and Charles. John lives in Washington and is a fixture in the Washington establishment. He is a "Mr. Go-To" if one needs help negotiating the Washington maze of government regulations. Charles, the youngest brother, lives in Sumter. He is the trained musician in the family. In recent years, he has been an oil consultant in Africa.

23

STATE BOARDS AND
COMMISSIONS DIVERSIFY

In 1969, the state of South Carolina had over 123 agencies. Each was governed by a board of directors or commissioners. In order to gain a seat on one these boards, it took an act of the legislature or an appointment by the governor. Prior to the Governor Robert E. McNair administration during the 1960s, no blacks served on any of the state agencies' boards. McNair took the first step toward integrating these various boards and commissions in 1969. First, he appointed two persons of color to the Department of Juvenile Corrections. He named Daisy D. Johnson head of the Urban League in Columbia and James L. Felder director of the South Carolina Voter Education Project. The same year, he named two blacks to the Juvenile After Care Board: Dr. Anna D. Reuben of Morris College in Sumter, who thirty years before was one of the founding members of the South Carolina Conference NAACP, and Reverend Al Holman, then president of the state NAACP. On the Board of Mental Health he placed Dr. J.C. Bull of Spartanburg. Herbert Fielding of Charleston was named to the Vocational Rehabilitation Board.

In 1970, Felder had to give up his seat on the Juvenile Correction Board after winning a seat in the House of Representatives. In his place, E. Perry Palmer of Sumter was named. There is a story behind Palmer's appointment. Prior to leaving the board, Felder had to participate in a board decision about which architectural firm would be hired to plan the new campus on Broad River Road for the Department of Youth Corrections. The board was divided two to two on the two firms that were being considered, with Felder holding out. Billie Goldsmith of Greenville, who chaired the board, pulled Felder aside and asked what they could do to get his vote. Felder said two things had to happen: one, he wanted to name his replacement on the board, and two, he wanted a black person to be named deputy director of the agency since there were no blacks in senior-level management on the staff. If these two things could happen, he would support the Goldsmith side. Goldsmith agreed, and they shook hands. Felder recommended Perry Palmer as his successor, and J.P. Neal, who had managed Felder's campaign, for the deputy director's position. In 1985, Palmer was elected chair of the board, a first for blacks to chair an agency board. J.P. Neal inaugurated a Sunday Morning Program on WIS TV called *AWARENESS*. It still airs today.

After Governor John C. West was elected in 1970, he created the Human Affairs Commission. He appointed Elliott E. Franks as chair of the board and Jim Clyburn as executive director, a first for both positions in state government.

In 1974, James Edwards, a Republican from Charleston, followed West in the governor's office. He made some minor appointments of blacks to serve on several boards but nothing earth shaking that captured the attention of the public.

Dick Riley of Greenville, one of the "Young Turks" who stood up to Sol Blatt, Edgar Brown and Marion Gressette in the General Assembly during the 1960s and '70s, was elected governor. Riley, who had served in the House and senate, made several important appointments of blacks to boards and commissions. First, he appointed Dr. C. Tyrone Gilmore of Spartanburg to chair the South Carolina Election Commission. Two other persons of color preceded Gilmore on the commission, Ernest A. Finney and Ruben Gray of Sumter. Both of them were elected to other positions of honor and had to step down because South Carolina does not permit dual office holding. Gilmore served eight years on the commission. He led the effort to automate the voting system, and as chair of the commission, he presided over the Allen Schaefer vote fraud case in the 1980s. Gilmore, an educator, became the first black superintendent of education in Spartanburg School District 7. He also has the distinction of being the first member of Omega Psi Phi Fraternity from South Carolina to be elected grand basileus of that national organization.

In 1980, Riley appointed Dr. Norma J. Givens to the Board of Financial Institutions. This is the agency that issues bank charters for state banks, consumer finance companies and check-cashing services and supervises the operations of these entities. Givens, a graduate of South Carolina State

University and the University of Georgia, is a Greer native. She served on the board from 1980 to 1988.

The South Carolina Highway Commission was an all-white, all-male body until Margaret Rush of Goose Creek was elected to that commission, where she served three terms. Rush later served as military liaison for Congressman Arthur Ravenel.

The Consumer Affairs Commission was chaired by Dr. Lonnie Randolph of Columbia. He also serves as the president of the state NAACP. The commission's director is a black female, Brandolyn Pinkston Thomas, who has served in that position for more than a decade.

Dr. Marianna W. Davis, a native of Orangeburg, was a pioneer on the Educational Television Commission. She served for many years and fostered the expansion of ETV into public schools and the TECH System. She is the author of many books.

In later years, many other blacks would serve on boards and commissions. Here, the emphasis has been on the early pioneers.

THUS FAR, THE FOCUS HAS been on persons who volunteer their time to serve on boards and commissions. However, there are three state agencies—the Employment Security Commission, the Public Service Commission and the Workers Compensation Commission—that pay compensation to their members. These coveted positions are sought after and lobbied for by individuals seeking them.

The Employment Security Commission is composed of three members who hear appeals from individuals who have been denied unemployment benefits. The commissioners are elected by the General Assembly for four-year terms. For many years, only former members of the General Assembly were elected by their colleagues to these positions. They are paid full-time salaries for what some say is part-time work. Two black former House and senate members, Sam Foster of Rock Hill and McKinley Washington of Charleston, have served on this commission. Foster also served as interim executive director of the commission. The new executive director is retired Major General Abraham Turner. Turner is a graduate of the South Carolina State University ROTC Program and rose to the rank of major general in the U.S. Army before retiring. In 2006, he was appointed commander of Fort Jackson, the army's largest training center, a first for a black soldier.

Another paying board is the Public Service Commission. It is a seven-member body that regulates all utilities, telephone, electricity, natural gas and intrastate railroads in the state. This commission is also elected by the General Assembly. The first black to serve on this commission was Marjorie Amos-Frazier of Charleston. She was elected in 1980 as the first black, first female, first non-legislator and first black to chair this body in 1990. After her retirement, Bill Saunders of Charleston replaced her on the commission. The third black to serve on this commission was Mignon Clyburn of Charleston, from 1998 to 2009, when she was appointed by President Obama to the Federal Communications Commission.

The third paying board, the Workers Compensation Commission, is made up of seven persons appointed by the governor and confirmed by the senate. Commissioners serve a six-year term. They are charged with enforcing the Workers Compensation laws. It is a quasi-judicial body and hears appeals from persons injured in the workplace due to no fault of their own. In 1985, Governor Riley appointed Milton Kimpson of Columbia and Rhienhart C. Brown of Charleston as the first blacks to serve on that commission. Kimpson served as the chief commissioner. The third person of color to serve was Bill Clyburn of Aiken. Clyburn, a cousin of Jim Clyburn, was later elected to the South Carolina House of Representatives from Aiken, and as of 2011, he chaired the legislative Black Caucus.

Blacks directing state agencies have been few. Jim Clyburn was the first, heading the Human Affairs Commission. He was followed there by Willis Ham of Charleston and Jesse Washington of Sumter. Ralph Haile is the present interim commissioner.

Donald Gist was appointed to the post of commissioner of the Commission on the Blind in 1990 and served until 1998. He was the first black to serve such an agency in South Carolina—and the nation, for that matter. His efforts led to the agency improving its standing from number forty-six to number one in ranking in the United States from 1995 to 1997.

Rick Wade of Lancaster was the first black to head the South Carolina Department of Alcohol and Drug Abuse. He was followed by Lee Cato at the agency. Wade is now a senior advisor to President Barack Obama.

At the South Carolina Probation Parole and Pardon Services, Steve Benjamin was the first person of color to serve. Sam Glover currently heads the agency. Benjamin was elected mayor of Columbia in 2010.

At the Wil Lou Gray Opportunity School, a state agency, where a twelve-member board is elected by the General Assembly for a four-year term, Wilhelmena McBride of Columbia served for twenty-eight years. When she stepped down in 2008, she handed over the seat to her sister, Doris M. Adams.

On the State Board of Education, where members are elected from the sixteen judicial circuits, James Blake of Marion was the first black to serve during the 1970s.

In the early years of the Commission on Higher Education, there were two staff persons who played a major role in shaping the commission's direction on equity for all races in the state. They were Julia E. Wells of Sumter and James L. Solomon.

24

OTHER BLACK ELECTED OFFICIALS

In 1960, Leroy Brown of Frogmore on St. Helena Island in Beaufort County won a seat on the Beaufort County Council, becoming the first black elected official in South Carolina since Reconstruction. His election ended a sixty-five-year drought of no blacks in public office.

In 1962, Charles Ross of Lincolnville was elected mayor, a first in South Carolina. He would become "the Dean" of black elected officials. By 1974, there were six black mayors in the state, and they hosted the Southern Conference of Black Mayors in Santee, where Silas Seabrook was mayor. Slowly in the 1960s, a trickle of black elected officials would surface. Willie Jefferson of Maysville in Sumter County won a seat on the town council in 1967 and became mayor in 1991. Beatrice Thompson of Anderson won an at-large seat on the city council in 1976. Later, she became the first woman and the first black to head the South Carolina Municipal Association. In the town of Carlisle in Union County, Janie Goree, a teacher at Sims High School in Union, was elected mayor in 1978.

In Georgetown, Maudest Squires won a seat on the Georgetown School Board and served from 1976 to 1984.

Slowly, blacks were beginning to win local political offices in spite of the fact that they had to run in at-large races for city and county positions. What started out as a trickle of black elected officials became a stream after 1987. In that year, the state NAACP, headed by its chief counsel, John Roy Harper II, launched a full assault on the at-large method of electing public officials in South Carolina. Over at Allen University, where Jim Felder chaired the Department of Business and Economics on the third floor of Chappelle

John Roy Harper II

Sunrise September 2, 1939   Sunset July 27, 2003

John Roy Harper was general
counsel for the state NAACP in
1987 and successfully argued the
cases for single-member districts at
the city, county council and school
board levels.

Hall, he provided space for the NAACP to set up a "war room" for drawing single-member district plans at the city, county and school board levels. Nelson B. Rivers III was executive director of the NAACP at that time, and he recruited Walker B. Solomon Jr., who had become very literate in drawing single-member district plans, to lead this effort. Rivers, Harper, Solomon and Felder spent long nights on the third floor of Chappelle Hall. This effort led to the creation of hundreds of single-member districts throughout South Carolina, and persons of color did not hesitate to run for public office in these newly created districts.

Since Leroy Brown's swearing-in in 1961, 926 blacks hold elective office in South Carolina at levels from the U.S. Congress to the local school board. Today, 2 blacks, Jim Clyburn and Tim Scott, serve in the U.S. Congress. In the South Carolina Senate, there are 9 men serving in a body of 46. One woman, Maggie Glover of Florence, served in that body during the 1990s. In the South Carolina House, there are 28 black men and women out of 124 seats. On county councils around the state, there are 128 black members. There are 12 sheriffs, 33 mayors, 372 city council members and 339 school board members.

At the mayoral level, most of the seats held by blacks are in small towns. However, in Spartanburg, James Talley became mayor of this predominately white city. Terrance Roberts did the same in Anderson. In 2010, Steve Benjamin was elected mayor of Columbia, and it was truly a moment for celebration. Chris King of Chester, who had run several times for public office, won the mayor's race and died after serving just four months in office. It was a very sad moment in Chester.

In countywide elected positions in recent years, black women have excelled in winning public office. There are eighteen women of color serving presently as county auditors, clerks of court, coroners, probate judges and treasurers (see the list that follows). On the other hand, black men have done well in races for sheriff. There are twelve black sheriffs out of forty-six presently serving (see list).

BLACK FEMALE COUNTY OFFICERS

Margaret Bostick, Clerk of Court, Jasper County
Pearl Brown, Treasurer, Williamsburg County
Gerzell Chaney, Treasurer, Allendale County
Rudell Gamble, Probate Judge, Williamsburg County
Verna Garvin, Treasurer, Jasper County
Henri Grant, Auditor, Allendale County
Patricia Grant, Clerk of Court, Colleton County
Hazel Holmes, Auditor, Jasper County
Samuetta Marshall, Coroner, Orangeburg County
Jeanette McBride, Clerk of Court, Richland County
Lucretia McCants, Auditor, Sumter County
Patricia Pringle, Auditor, Clarendon County
Carolina Richardson, Treasurer, Sumter County
Beaulah Roberts, Clerk of Court, Clarendon County
Loretta Washington, Treasurer, Georgetown County
Alma White, Clerk of Court, Georgetown County
Carolyn Williams, Clerk of Court, Williamsburg County
Teresa Williams, Auditor, Hampton County

BLACK SHERIFFS

Lee Brown, Hampton County
Francis Coath, Allendale County
Anthony Dennis, Sumter County
Adell Dobey, Edgefield County
C.H. Goodwin, Abbeville County

E.J. Melvin, Lee County
George H. Reid, McCormick County
Benjamin Riley, Jasper County
William C. Simon, Marlboro County
Kelvin Washington, Williamsburg County
Larry Williams, Orangeburg County
Herman Young, Fairfield County

While the local police, highway patrol, sheriff and SLED agents catch and arrest the bad guys, it is the solicitor who prosecutes them. The solicitor is an elected official. Prior to 1973, there were no black prosecutors at any level in South Carolina. Solicitor John Foard of Richland County changed that with the appointment of Jim Felder as an assistant solicitor of the Fifth Judicial Circuit in February 1973. In Charleston that same year, Daniel Martin Sr. was appointed assistant solicitor. Others would also be appointed. In Greenville, Fletcher Smith was appointed; in Columbia, Lynne Rogers got the appointment. The first black to win a solicitor race was Ralph Wilson in the Fifteenth Judicial Circuit, which covers Horry and Georgetown Counties. He served from 1992 to 2000. In 2010, Ernest "Chip" Finney of Sumter and Dan Johnson of Columbia won solicitor positions, becoming the second and third persons of color to win these appointments. Finney won the Third Judicial Circuit seat, which covers Sumter, Lee, Clarendon and Williamsburg Counties. Johnson won the Fifth Judicial Circuit seat, covering Richland and Kershaw Counties.

25

THEY ALSO RAN

There have been blacks who sought statewide and lesser public office and did not win. Thomas D. Broad Sr., of Columbia, and Reverend J.C. McTeer ran for governor and lieutenant governor, respectively, in 1970 on the United Citizens Party ticket without success.

Dr. Claude Stephenson of Kingstree ran for the Sixth District congressional seat in 1968 against longtime congressman John L. McMillian. McMillian was chair of the District of Columbia Committee, and in effect, he was mayor of D.C. The District of Columbia did not have home rule at that time, and McMillian was the "Boss." Stephenson received a lot of financial support from D.C. residents who wanted to see McMillian defeated. Stevenson did not win, but the race softened up McMillian and set the stage for John Jennerett to defeat him four years later.

Matthew J. Perry of Columbia was chief counsel for the NAACP in 1974, when he decided to enter the race for the Second District congressional seat against Floyd Spence. Perry did not win, but his well-organized campaign frightened Spence and others in the Republican Party to the point that Senator Strom Thurmond recommended Perry to President Gerald Ford for a seat on the U.S. Court of Military Appeals. Thurmond's action was viewed by many as a way to remove Perry as a future threat to Spence's Second District seat.

Following Perry's effort to unseat Spence, Ken Moseley, a faculty member at South Carolina State College, picked up the mantle and ran aggressive, spirited races in 1982 and 1984 for the Second District congressional seat. He won the Democratic Party primary both times but lost in the general election both times.

Down in Charleston in the First Congressional District, in 1968 George Payton had the gall to take on Congressman L. Mendel Rivers, chair of the Armed Services Committee. While Payton did not win his protest race, it showed that blacks in the First Congressional District were not happy with Rivers's representation.

A perennial black candidate in the First Congressional District has been Ben Frazier, who has run more than six times for that seat in the past twenty years. Frazier worked on Rivers's Washington staff for years. Upon Rivers's death, Frazier returned to Charleston and began pursuing the seat. His last run for the seat was in 2010 against another black, Tim Scott, who ran as a Republican and won.

In recent statewide races, the Reverend Fred Dawson of Charleston ran for comptroller general in 1986 on the United Citizens Party ticket.

In 1994, Milton Kimpson made a try at the secretary of state position. He ran a good race, but some say South Carolina was not ready for a black man to hold a constitutional office. Rick Wade followed Kimpson in a run for the office in 2002. He made a valiant effort but came up short.

Steve Benjamin ran for attorney general in 2002 at the same time Wade was running for secretary of state. He, too, came up short after a very spirited race. He was elected mayor of Columbia in 2010.

Black candidates ran for the U.S. Senate as early as 1944, when Osceola McKaine of Sumter took on Olin D. Johnson in that race. He did not win, but it opened the eyes of blacks in South Carolina and energized and inspired them to register and vote.

In 2010, an unknown black candidate from Manning, Alvin Greene, won the Democratic Party primary for the U.S. Senate seat. It was a bizarre election. Greene's opponent, Judge Victor Rawls, who was known statewide (and white), filed a protest with the South Carolina Democratic Party. Hearings were held, and the party ruled that Greene won it fair and square. Greene never campaigned, had no staff, did not advertise and won 60 percent of the vote in the primary. In the November general election, he lost to Jim Demint, the Republican incumbent.

In the 2004 general election, Tee Ferguson, a former judge and legislator from Spartanburg, ran for the U.S. Senate on the United Citizens Party ticket.

In 1990, Theo Mitchell, state senator from Greenville, was the Democratic Party candidate for governor. He lost to fellow Greenville native Carroll Campbell, the Republican candidate. Mitchell was also the lieutenant governor's candidate in 1994.

From Peaceful Protests to Groundbreaking Rulings

Kevin Gray mounted a write-in campaign for governor in 2002 without success. Dr. Morgan Reeves ran for governor on the United Citizens Party ticket in 2010.

There were many others who ran for public office and set the stage for today's black officeholders. In Richland County, Hemphill Pride ran for the House of Representatives and senate. Alvin Portee, a perennial candidate for coroner, has run more than six times. Modjeska M. Simkins ran for city council, House of Representatives and school board in the early days. She said it was just to shake things up.

26

BLACK DEMOCRATS AND BLACK REPUBLICANS

Following the emancipation of the slaves by President Abraham Lincoln and the passage of Fifteenth Amendment that allowed black males to vote, these newly freed slaves became part of the Republican Party. All of the Reconstruction legislators were Republicans. This was a way for ex-slaves to show their gratitude to Lincoln for having freed them. The presidential election of 1876 and the deal that was struck took away all of the political gains made by blacks. The white Democrats took control of the political process and subjected blacks to a new kind of servitude, with black codes and Jim Crow laws.

Blacks did not participate in elections again until Franklin D. Roosevelt ran in 1932 as a Democrat. The few blacks who were able to vote supported Roosevelt. He appointed a few blacks to positions in his administration. The most notable one was Mary McLeod Bethune of Maysville in Sumter County. She became very close to Eleanor Roosevelt, the president's wife, who supported the black cause and served on the NAACP National Board of Directors. In spite of these connections, blacks were not able to participate in the South Carolina Democratic Party primary until 1948, following the *Elmore v. Rice* decision. After the Elmore decision, it was still difficult to participate in the Democratic Party primary. In 1956, some of those blacks who still supported the Republican Party went to the Republican Convention in California. The delegation was led by I.S. Leevy, Columbia mortician and businessman. Reverend I.D. Newman, who became one of the icons of the civil rights struggle in South Carolina, was part of that delegation.

From Peaceful Protests to Groundbreaking Rulings

There was still an allegiance to the Republic Party by some of the old-line blacks because of Lincoln until the 1960 presidential election between John F. Kennedy and Richard Nixon. When the Kennedy brothers made a call to a Georgia jail seeking the release of Dr. Martin Luther King, many black voters moved to the Democratic Party. Following Dr. King's release, his father, Daddy King, as he was affectionately known, went on national TV and radio and announced that he would be supporting the Democratic nominee, John F. Kennedy. Daddy King had been a solid Republican all of his life, but the jail incident and the lack of response from Nixon, the Republican nominee, changed him.

Blacks were further enticed to support the Democrats following President Lyndon Johnson's pushing the 1964 Civil Rights Act and the 1965 Voting Rights Act through Congress. Those two instances moved 90 percent of the black vote to the Democratic column. Many felt they had paid their debt to Lincoln. When President Johnson appointed Thurgood Marshall to the U.S. Supreme Court, the act solidified black support for the Democratic Party.

When President Johnson signed the 1965 Voting Rights Act, he said, "I know I am doing the right thing, but I am sure we are going to lose the southern white Democrats." His prophecy was correct. Immediately, Senator Strom Thurmond bolted from the Democratic Party and switched to the Republican Party. He was followed by Congressman Floyd Spence of Lexington, who was a Democrat. In the South Carolina House of Representatives, there were only two Republicans at that time. White Democrats began switching parties or were beaten by Republican candidates running against them citing the illegality of the Voting Rights Act. This is when the South began to switch to the Republican Party. Southerners were angry with President Johnson for the passage of the Civil Rights and Voting Rights Acts.

In 1968, President Johnson declined to run for a second term. Richard Nixon adopted a southern strategy that was put together by Harry Dent of St. Matthews, South Carolina. Part of that strategy was to encourage whites to run as Republicans. The solidly Democratic South began to shift to a solidly Republican South that seemed bent on reversing the gains blacks had made.

In 1974, redistricting opened the door for more blacks to get elected, but it also opened the door for more white Republicans by way of single-member districts.

Nixon appointed some blacks to his administration and gave out some government contracts. These acts attracted some black business types. Bob Brown of Winston-Salem, North Carolina, became the "Godfather" of this project. He brought aboard a young man named Armstrong Williams of Marion, South Carolina. Williams, a graduate of South Carolina State College, was brought on to recruit blacks for the Republican Party. A big catch for the Republicans was Dr. Charles H. Thomas of Orangeburg. Dr. Thomas was a professor at South Carolina State College, president of the South Carolina Voter Education Project and president of the Orangeburg Branch NAACP. He was also on the short list of candidates for the presidency of South Carolina State College in 1968 following the ouster of Dr. B.C. Turner. When the board selected Dr. Maceo Nance over Thomas, he was disappointed, and he accepted an appointment by President Nixon to serve as the Equal Opportunity Officer for the U.S. Postal Service in Washington, D.C.

Another big catch for the Republicans was Thomas Moss of Orangeburg. Moss was very active in the civil rights struggle in South Carolina. He replaced Jim Felder as executive director of the South Carolina Voter Education Project when Felder was elected to the South Carolina House of Representatives in 1970. Moss had statewide connections and knew all the black elected officials. Senator Thurmond saw value in that, and he hired Moss as his state coordinator for constituent services. Moss spent thirty years with Thurmond. He was the first black staffer to serve in any of the southern congressmen's offices.

Nathaniel Abraham is a longtime Republican who has published newspapers in Columbia for the past fifty years. He is considered the dean of black publishers in the state. He was a mentee of the late Modjeska Simkins. He was on the scene the night of the Orangeburg Massacre and pleaded with Chief Pete Strom to not let any of the armed personnel fire their weapons. His plea fell on deaf ears, and the casualties were three deaths and twenty-seven wounded students.

Others who climbed aboard the Republican train included Redfern II and Isaac Washington, publishers of *Black News*, a newspaper with wide circulation in the state. They received government contracts to do grass cutting on military bases in the southeastern United States. Brothers Willie and Freddie Williams were recipients of similar contracts. Many others enjoyed these newfound opportunities. They would tell you it was not about ideology but just plain business.

Others who have identified with the Republican Party in the last twenty-five years include Stephon Edwards of Orangeburg; Pat Flack of Anderson; the Pickering family of Charleston; and Frank Washington, Lee Cato, Joseph Strickland, Bobby Pearson, Clarence Davis, Reggie Lloyd, Charles Derrick and Milton Davenport, all of Columbia.

Active participants in party affairs include Bishop Johnny Smith of Greenville, who chaired the Black Republican Council. Celestine White Parker of Orangeburg and Columbia chaired the Minority Development Council. Willis Ham of Columbia was co-chair of the RE-Elect Governor Carroll Campbell Committee in 1990. Earl Brown of Columbia is an assistant to Congressman Joe Wilson of the Second Congressional District.

In 2008, blacks garnered two high-profile positions in the Republican Party. Glenn McCall of Rock Hill was elected national committeeman from South Carolina to the National Republican Committee. At the same time, Tim Scott of Charleston won a seat in the South Carolina House of Representatives as a Republican for the first time since Reconstruction. Scott had served on the Charleston County Council prior to his House win. In the 2010 elections, Scott reached a higher profile when he won the First District congressional seat and became the first black to reach Congress as a Republican since Reconstruction.

Scott's path to victory was interesting. He had to defeat four white candidates in the Republican primary. Two of these candidates were sons of former governors Strom Thurmond and Carroll Campbell. There was a runoff between Scott and Paul Thurmond. Scott won. The First Congressional District runs along the coast and includes most of Charleston County, Georgetown County and Horry County; it is a majority-white district.

BACK TO BLACK DEMOCRATS. In 1969, four years after the passage of the 1965 Voting Rights Act, blacks were still having trouble getting elected to office because of the Democratic Party's full-slate law. The full-slate law required that voters cast ballots for the full number of positions in each race. It meant that in a race for legislators in which five seats were available, a black person had to vote for five persons even if he or she only wanted to vote for the lone black on the ballot. If you did not vote for five persons, your ballot would be voided or not counted. Further, it meant that blacks had to vote for white candidates whom they did not know or want. Whites did not vote for black candidates, so a person of color did not get enough votes to be elected.

To counter this Democratic Party system, in 1969 a new party was organized to bypass this system. The new party was called the United Citizen Party (UCP). Led by Jim Clyburn, the organizers included Jim Solomon, Ed Day, John Roy Harper, Jim Felder and others. While the UCP was going through the final steps of organizing, the South Carolina Democratic Party appointed its first black staff person, Joel Ward, in December 1969. Jim

Clyburn stated to a news reporter, "The appointment of Ward is obviously a Democratic move to show blacks that they need not resort to a splinter party to have a political voice." Some of the more enlightened whites heard Clyburn loud and clear. In the spring of 1970, leading up to the June primary, young white Democrats in Columbia and Charleston began to reach out to black candidates seeking seats in the South Carolina House of Representatives. Clyburn and Fielding in Charleston and Felder and Johnson in Columbia won the Democratic primary that year. Following the elections, the United Citizens Party was put on the shelf to be used at another time.

27

HBCUs

There are eight Historical Black Colleges and Universities (HBCUs) in South Carolina. Six of them—Allen University, Benedict College, Claflin University, Clinton Junior College, Morris College and Voorhees College—are private. The other two, Denmark Technical College and South Carolina State University, are publicly funded. Three other historical black colleges—Friendship Junior College, Harbison Junior College and King Memorial College—no longer exist.

FRIENDSHIP JUNIOR COLLEGE

Friendship was founded in 1891 by the Chester and York Counties Missionary Baptist Association, led by Dr. M.P. Hall, in Rock Hill, South Carolina. It operated until 1982, when lack of sufficient operating funds forced the school to close. It filed for bankruptcy, and much of its assets were sold to pay creditors and the federal government for funds incorrectly spent. In 1983, the two County Baptist Conventions received a loan from Benedict College in the amount of $166,000 to purchase back land from the bankruptcy court. That was done, and today there are plans in progress to build a multipurpose structure on the site that will house the two Baptist conventions, a daycare for adults and children and an assembly area for reunions, weddings and conventions. The name of the facility will be the Gouldlock Building, named in honor of Dr. James H. Gouldlock, who served for forty-two years as president of Friendship Junior College. Friendship was the campus from which the "Rock Hill 9" emerged and staged the sit-ins in Rock Hill in 1960.

HARBISON JUNIOR COLLEGE

Harbison Institute was founded in Abbeville, South Carolina, in 1892. It later moved to Columbia in 1911 and remained there until it closed in 1958. Affiliated with the Presbyterian Church, it was a feeder school for Johnson C. Smith University in Charlotte, North Carolina. Its early curriculum focused on agriculture. One of its more famous graduates is Harold R. Boulware, the NAACP state conference lawyer who worked on the *Briggs v. Elliott* school desegregation case with Thurgood Marshall. He became a family court judge. Midlands Technical College's Harbison Campus is the present-day institution of higher learning on the old Harbison Campus. Boulware is buried on the campus in a private cemetery.

KING MEMORIAL COLLEGE

The third HBCU that is no longer around is King Memorial College. Founded in 1976 by Dr. B.J. Glover, the school closed in 1979.

Dr. Glover had served as president of Allen University in two different periods. His last tenure ended in a dispute with the board of trustees, and he left. He still had a vision to continue his career in higher education, so he rented a building at the corner of Laurel and Henderson Streets in Columbia and started enrolling students. Without accreditation and unable to qualify for federal funding, the school closed its doors in 1979.

ALLEN UNIVERSITY

Founded in 1870 by former slaves, Allen was the first institution of higher learning to come into existence through the efforts of persons of color to teach persons of color. In its early years, when it provided training for all ages, one could enter in the first grade and leave prepared to teach, preach or plead cases in the court. Allen University is the only institution of higher learning named for the Right Reverend Richard Allen, the first consecrated bishop and acknowledged founder of the African Methodist Episcopal Church.

Allen suffered some hard times. When the school hired two white professors in the 1950s, the state Department of Education pulled its teacher certification authorization. A revolving door of presidents and bishops in the

1970s caused further difficulties. Misappropriation of funds and failing to pay withholding taxes to IRS almost closed the doors of the school that was once the flagship of HBCUs in South Carolina.

Dr. B.J. Glover, in his second presidency at Allen, saved the school from extinction in 1974, when he sought assistance from Senator Strom Thurmond to keep the IRS from placing a lien on the school's property. Thurmond responded to Glover's request, and the lien just went away. Glover thanked Thurmond by bestowing on him a doctor of humane letters degree. Glover left in 1976, and Allen took a nosedive, financially, again.

When Bishop Fred James arrived in 1984 and took over as chair of the board, Allen was down to two hundred students, it was indebted to the federal government, faculty had not been paid in months, creditors threatened lawsuits, the power company was about to turn the lights off and half the buildings on campus were boarded up. Some said Allen was in intensive care and waiting for the undertaker to pick up the body.

Bishop James, an Allen graduate and native of Prosperity, declared, "Allen University must rise again." He leaned on the five hundred AME churches in South Carolina and demanded that they do more to support Allen financially and to help recruit students.

Dr. Sylvia Swinton, an Allen graduate, and Mrs. Fannie Phelps Adams had served as interim presidents when Bishop James arrived. They were holding on until help arrived. James brought with him Dr. Collie Coleman as his new president. Coleman had worked under James at Shorter College, another AME college in Arkansas, and was successful in gaining accreditation for that school. Coleman lured away from Claflin University Dr. Karen A. Woodfaulk to serve as his academic officer. Bishop James prevailed on one of his mentees from his Sumter days, James L. Felder, to chair the Department of Business and Economics and do double duty as chair of the Accreditation Committee. Felder had been teaching courses on a volunteer basis in the Business Department because the school had no funds to pay him.

Fast-forward to 1988. Allen was out of intensive care, enrollment was up, debts were under control and the school was announcing the building of a shopping center on Taylor Street on the site of the old Hurst football field, where the Allen Yellow Jackets played football in their heyday. In 1991, after resolving some old debt issues with the U.S. Department of Education, Allen University was granted full accreditation by SACS.

In 1992, Bishop James had served the two four-year terms that are allowed under AME church rules, and he had to rotate out. He was replaced by Bishop John Hurst Adams, a native of Columbia, who literally grew up on the campus of Allen because his father, Reverend E.A. Adams, was an administrator at Allen for over forty years. Bishop Adams is a graduate of Johnson C. Smith University.

Adams launched a building and restoration program. With the aid of Congressman Jim Clyburn, he obtained a $1.6 million grant from the National Park Service to renovate Arnett Hall, the 110-year-old building that once was one of the nation's most endangered historical sites. Adams was also able to secure funding for a badly needed physical education building that bears his name: the Bishop John Hurst Adams Gymnatorium.

Bishop Adams was replaced in 2000 by Bishop Henry Belin Jr. During his four years as presiding prelate of the Seventh AME Episcopal District and chair of the Allen University Board of Trustees, he can best be described as a caretaker of the institution.

In 2004, Bishop Preston Warren Williams III was assigned to South Carolina by the General Conference of the AME Church. His first action was to visit each of the six hundred AME churches in South Carolina, a first for all the bishops who have passed through the state. He restructured the board of trustees at Allen and brought on some business and corporate individuals. Along with President Charles Young, he continued the building efforts started by Bishop Adams. Two new residence halls, male and female, were built. Portions of the shopping center on Taylor Street were retrofitted to create the new Center for Educational Excellence. It houses a state-of-the-art dining facility, Career Development Center, Bookstore and Alumni Center. Renovations on Gibbs Science Hall, Chappelle Administration Building and the Sons of Allen Chapel were completed. The total cost of these projects was $29.3 million.

Alumni and supporters of Allen University point with pride to the achievements of its graduates. Eight alumni have gone on to become presidents of colleges and universities. Twelve were elevated to bishops in the AME Church. Another nine have served or are serving in the South Carolina legislature. They are, in the South Carolina Senate, Kay Patterson, Ralph Anderson and Clemente Pinckney, and in the South Carolina House, Floyd Breeland, Joe E. Brown, William Clyburn, Mack Hines, Daniel Martin Sr. and DeWitt Williams.

On March 29, 2012, Dr. Pamela M. Wilson was inaugurated as the first female president of Allen University. She is a native of Fairfield County and a Baptist, the first in the school's history.

BENEDICT COLLEGE

While Allen University was founded by newly freed slaves, Benedict was founded by a white northern philanthropist, Bathsheba Benedict, a Rhode Island native, in 1870. It opened its doors on an eighty-acre plantation in Columbia and was named Benedict Institute. The goal of Mrs. Benedict and the Baptist Home Mission was to educate emancipated slaves.

Dr. J.J. Starks was Benedict's first black president. Starks had served as president at Seneca Junior College and Morris College. He brought years of experience when he arrived in 1930 and served until his death in 1944.

In 1967, Orangeburg native Dr. Benjamin Payton was selected to head the school, and he served until 1972. Off campus, Payton was selected to be a member of the Electoral College from South Carolina for the 1968 presidential election. This was a first for blacks in the state. Payton enticed Greenwood native and higher education icon Dr. Benjamin E. Mays to join the board of trustees, where he served from 1973 to 1984. Payton began a building program on which his successor, Dr. Henry Ponder, expanded from 1973 to 1984.

Following the Ponder administration, Dr. Marshall Grigsby served from 1984 to 1993. Some questionable financial matters caused a cloud to form over him, and he left.

Enter Dr. David H. Swinton, who launched a massive building program that included a student center, a stadium and an athletic field on Two Notch Road and brought back football after a thirty-year hiatus. Off campus, Swinton joined a group of investors who purchased the assets of the Victory Savings Bank when it went under and established a new bank, South Carolina Community Bank, with branches in Eastover, Orangeburg and Sumter. The main office and a branch are in Columbia.

Some notable alumni of Benedict include Modjeska M. Simkins, Dr. Leroy Walker, Major General Matthew Zimmerman and I.S. Leevy Johnson Esq., to name a few.

For more information on Benedict College, read *The Enduring Dream: History of Benedict College* by Dr. Marianna W. Davis.

CLAFLIN UNIVERSITY

Claflin was founded in 1869 by Methodist missionaries to prepare newly freed slaves to take their rightful place as full American citizens. The first three presidents were white northern missionaries. The first black president was Dr. Joseph B. Randolph. He had served at two HBCUs: Texas College and Wiley College. He placed emphasis on a liberal arts education. He served from 1922 until 1944. Dr. J.J. Scabrook replaced Randolph and stayed until 1955. During his tenure, the endowment increased, and the college was accredited by the SACS in 1948.

Dr. H.V. Manning became Claflin's sixth president in 1956. He was a Methodist minister and former associate professor at the school. Under his leadership, the faculty was strengthened, and the endowment increased. The physical plant was expanded.

The seventh president of Claflin was Dr. Oscar Rogers Jr. He served from 1984 to 1994. During his administration, the Grace Thomas Kennedy building was constructed, the financial base of the college was improved and two capital campaigns were completed. He also commissioned a master plan to guide campus development into the twenty-first century.

The eighth and current president, Dr. Henry Tisdale, a native of Williamsburg County and a graduate of Claflin, came aboard in 1994. Prior to assuming the presidency at Claflin, Tisdale served as senior vice-president and chief academic officer at Delaware State University in Dover, Delaware. Upon arrival, he declared that "academic excellence" would be the number one priority for Claflin. He established the Honor College and the Center for Excellence in science and math. He established graduate programs in business administration, a master's of science in BioTech and the master's in education. Facilities enhancement included the construction of the Living and Learning Center, Legacy Plaza, the student residential center, the music center and the new University Chapel. Claflin is now recognized as one of the premier liberal arts institutions in the nation.

Claflin gave birth to South Carolina State College. An act of the South Carolina General Assembly on March 12, 1872, designated the State Agriculture and Mechanical Institute as part of Claflin. Claflin received direct appropriations from the legislature to support the institute until 1896, when the General Assembly passed an act separating the institute from Claflin and establishing a new school that eventually became South Carolina State College.

Following Reconstruction in 1874, Claflin had a Law Department that was headed by the Honorable Jonathan J. Wright, the first black South Carolina Supreme Court justice. His graduates were admitted to the South Carolina bar without any problem.

For more information on Claflin University, read *Men of Vision: Claflin College and Her Presidents* by Vivian Glover.

MORRIS COLLEGE

Morris College was founded in 1908 in Sumter by the South Carolina Baptist Education and Missionary Convention. Its purpose was described as being "for the Christian and Intellectual Training for Negro Youth." In the beginning, the school provided training at every level—elementary and high school, and even college courses were offered. The early curriculum was the preparation for teaching and preaching. Today, the curriculum includes over twenty majors.

One of the early presidents of the school was Dr. J.J. Starks. He started the ball rolling and moved on to Benedict College. The college survived the Depression and World War II, and in 1948, Dr. O.R. Ruben took over the reins of the presidency and served until his death in 1970. The four years following Ruben's death were turbulent ones for the college. The college had been administered by a series of interim presidents and committees.

In July 1974, the board of trustees hired Dr. Luns Richardson as president. Richardson, a native of Hartsville, worked his way through Benedict as a student. He brought experience as an administrator that he gained at Allen University, Benedict College, Denmark Tech and Voorhees College. Upon entering the president's office on July 1, 1974, he found a $450,000 operating deficit in its budget, of which $300,000 was payroll taxes due to IRS. The buildings were badly in need of repairs, and the school had only 240 students enrolled the previous semester. The female students did not have satisfactory living quarters, and the college needed a women's dormitory. And to top it all, Morris was not accredited, which prevented the school from being eligible for grants and other donations from the government and foundations. It also presented a problem for graduates to compete for jobs.

Undertaking what Richardson called "the greatest challenge I have ever faced," he proceeded immediately to eliminate the deficit by setting up a payment plan with the IRS. He then met with creditors to work out a payment plan or write off the debt entirely. He contacted representatives for the SACS, an agency he had come in contact with during his days at Benedict and Allen. Four years later, in 1978, Morris College was accredited.

In 1982, the college was accepted as a member of the United Negro College Fund, the nation's largest and most successful black fundraising organization. Dr. Richardson oversaw a building program that has tripled the size of the campus since his arrival.

A great milestone for Dr. Richardson and Morris College was reached on January 7, 2009, when a former student, Reverend Solomon Jackson, pastor of the Shiloh Baptist Church in Columbia, donated $10 million to the school. It was the largest single gift in the history of Morris. Jackson won the Power Ball Lottery jackpot, which consisted of $260 million, and he wanted to help with the education of students at Morris College.

Dr. Luns Richardson has the distinction of being the longest-serving president of any college in South Carolina. He has been at Morris College for thirty-seven years as of this writing (2012).

For more about Morris College, read *Morris College: A Noble Journey* by Marsey Vareen-Gordon and Janice Smith Clayton.

CLINTON JUNIOR COLLEGE

Clinton Junior College was one of many schools established by the AME Zion Church during Reconstruction to help eradicate illiteracy among freedmen. Located in Rock Hill, South Carolina, it has operated continuously for 116 years. In 1894, presiding elder Nero L. Crockett and Reverend W.M. Robinson founded Clinton Institute and named it for the presiding bishop at that time, Bishop Isom Caleb Clinton.

Incorporated as Clinton Normal and Industrial Institute on June 22, 1909, the school was authorized to grant state teacher certificates. By the late 1940s, the college attracted 225 students per year and owned nineteen acres of land, several buildings and equipment valued at $7 million.

Under Dr. Sallie V. Moreland, who retired in 1994 after forty-nine years of service, the school's charter was amended to create Clinton Junior College. When Dr. Cynthia L.M. Russell assumed leadership, the school prepared for accreditation, and it was attained during the tenure of Dr. Elaine Johnson Copeland.

During the first decade of the twenty-first century, under the leadership of Dr. Copeland, the college has received over $4 million in grants from the U.S. Department of Energy, the South Carolina Education Department, the Lutz Foundation and the AME Zion Church.

DENMARK TECHNICAL COLLEGE

Denmark Technical College is located in Denmark, South Carolina. It was created and authorized by the General Assembly in 1947. It was originally called Area Trade School for Negroes. At its inception, the institution functioned under the authority of the South Carolina Department of Education and was mandated to educate black citizens in various trades. Following World War II, many black veterans flocked to the school to learn barbering, electricity, heating and air conditioning, brick laying and related trades. Utilizing the GI Bill, many of them became craftsmen and artisans.

In 1969, control of the Denmark Area Trade School was transferred to the South Carolina Advisory Committee for Technical Training, which acted under the State Board for Technical and Comprehensive Education. During the same year, the name of the college was changed to Denmark Technical Education Center. In 1979, the institution was accredited by the SACS and assumed its present designation as Denmark Technical College.

The campus stands on fifty-three acres of land located fifty miles south of Columbia. Its primary service area consists of Bamberg, Barnwell and Allendale Counties, with a mandate to serve students from throughout the state. It offers associate degrees and certificates in certain crafts. It sits across the road from Voorhees College.

Voorhees College

The history of Voorhees College starts with Elizabeth Wright, who at the age of twenty-three was a little older than today's Voorhees students when she came to Bamberg County, South Carolina. A native of Georgia, Wright found her inspiration while studying at Booker T. Washington's Tuskegee Institute. She said that her time at Tuskegee gave her a mission in life of being "the same type of women as Mr. Washington was a man." Knowing the importance of education, she moved to rural Denmark and started the first school in the area for blacks. She survived threats, attacks and arson. She went back to Tuskegee to finish her degree before returning to South Carolina to try again. Undeterred and envisioning a better education for blacks, she founded Denmark Industrial School in 1897, modeling it after Tuskegee. New Jersey philanthropist Ralph Voorhees and his wife donated $5,000 to buy the land, allowing the school to open in 1902 with Wright as its principal. It was the only high school for blacks in the area.

In 1924, the Episcopal Church began supporting the school, and that relationship continues today. In 1947, the school became Voorhees School and Junior College. In 1962, it was accredited as four-year Voorhees College.

In 1969, Voorhees made national headlines. There were two episodes of student uprisings on campus. Voorhees students, like other students around the country, were beginning to become aware of their heritage and were demanding that more emphasis be placed on teaching it. The students organized a committee called the Black Awareness Coordinating Committee (BACC). Dr. John F. Potts was president of the college at that time when several students, armed with weapons, took over the library in Wilkinson Hall. They covered the windows with newspaper and renamed the library Malcolm X University. They issued the following demands:

> *More books on black studies in library*
> *A resident physician and nurse on campus*
> *Minimum wages for kitchen and ground maintenance employees*
> *Cease purchasing goods from white merchants downtown*
> *Better housing for on-campus living*
> *Reinstate 60 students flunked by a white professor*
> *Amnesty for all protesters*

The South Carolina National Guard was called in and aimed its tanks at the library. Dr. Potts agreed to the demands, and the students left the library without any casualties. This occurred on April 28, 1969, and the campus was closed for two weeks. Upon reopening, graduation exercises took place that June, and the students went home for the summer. While away, thirty-six students were charged with common law rioting and trespassing. Eight of the thirty-six were indicted. They called themselves the "Voorhees 8." They were: Alvin Evans, Oliver Francis, Gerald Albert, Cecil Raysor, James Epps, Michael Moore, Sam Mintz and James Bryant.

Upon returning in the fall of 1969, Dr. Potts resigned, citing health reasons. Harry Graham was appointed interim president. Isaac W. Williams, NAACP field secretary, interceded in an effort to get some of the charges dismissed against the students. The trespassing charges were dismissed, but the rioting charges stayed.

In February 1970, the students staged a boycott of classes, citing the fact that their spring 1969 demands had not been acted upon. The administration closed the campus for six weeks. Some students refused to leave. Governor Robert McNair, remembering what had happened at South Carolina State College two years earlier, did not want another massacre on his watch. He dispatched Elliott Franks III of the Columbia Urban League and Jim Felder of the South Carolina Voter Education Project to Denmark to try to convince the remaining students to leave. They were able to convince all except two students to leave. Jerry Gambrell of Charleston and Willie

Williams of Chester were arrested when the National Guard rolled on campus in the early morning hours.

In the summer of 1970, the Voorhees 8 went on trial. They were all convicted. On appeal to the South Carolina Supreme Court, the cases were affirmed. Raysor and Evans received two-year sentences, and the others received eighteen months. Fred Henderson Moore of Charleston and Matthew J. Perry of Columbia represented the students.

Other student leaders involved in these episodes on the campus included Raymond Singleton of Sumter and Clyde Holliday. The charges against them were dropped.

As of 2010, the president of Voorhees was Dr. Cleveland Sellers Jr. He is a graduate of Voorhees High School and an icon of the civil rights movement. He was director of communications for the SNCC. As a victim of the Orangeburg Massacre, he was prosecuted for rioting and sentenced to a year of hard labor. Later, he was pardoned, earned a doctoral degree and directed the African American Studies Program at USC before accepting the presidency at Voorhees College. One of his sons, Bakari, was elected to the South Carolina House of Representatives at age twenty-one and represents Bamberg County, the home of Voorhees College.

SOUTH CAROLINA STATE UNIVERSITY

In 1896, the U.S. Supreme Court handed down its infamous decision *Plessey v. Ferguson*, which confirmed Jim Crow laws and the black codes that said blacks were not equal to whites and could be treated differently. It was the beginning of the separate-but-equal doctrine that would last until 1954, when the U.S. Supreme Court overruled the decision in *Brown v. Board of Education*. Also in 1896, the white power structure of South Carolina, in an effort to show that it was treating its black citizens "equally," allowed the General Assembly to pass an act creating South Carolina A&M College in Orangeburg. It was already sending funds to Claflin University to assist in the education of freedmen. However, this action would create a new school on a 126-acre site next door to Claflin.

The first president was Thomas E. Miller, a former black congressman, and he held the post for fifteen years. During Miller's tenure, with his faculty of fifteen, the college's physical plant consisted of 133 acres, eight small buildings, a dairy herd and a few other farm animals. Because of the meager facilities, the academic institution was given primary dibs on logs hewn from the campus forest. These same logs would later be made into lumber for building the first classrooms and dormitories.

Upon Miller's retirement, Dr. Robert Shaw Wilkinson, a Charleston native and professor of physics at the college, was elevated to the presidency. His twenty-one-year administration witnessed an increase in faculty and student enrollment, the establishment of funding from federal and state sources, an expansion in the building program, a cooperative working relationship with Clemson University and Claflin, the initiation of a state summer school and the celebration of the college's twenty-fifth birthday.

The death of President Wilkinson on March 13, 1932, catapulted Dr. Miller F. Whittaker into acting president and, subsequently, president in May 1932. The milestones achieved under Dr. Whittaker from 1932 to 1949 were the establishment of the law school, the extension school with units in fifteen counties and the ROTC program and the college appearing on the SACS' list of approved colleges. Whittaker died of heart failure at age fifty-two. Some say he worked himself to death.

Upon Whittaker's death in 1950, Dr. Benner C. Turner, dean of the law school, became the fourth president of the college. During his watch, there was rapid growth in undergraduate and graduate enrollment. Faculty and staff increased, and the number of faculty with terminal degrees went up. Major improvements included the construction of the Academic Building, more dormitories for men and women and a cafeteria. New walkways, drives, roads and attractive landscaping added to the beauty of the campus and the comfort of its inhabitants. Following two student uprisings on the campus in 1957 and 1967, Dr. Turner was forced into retirement.

On June 23, 1968, Dr. Maceo Nance Jr. succeeded to the presidency after a one-year tenure as interim president. Dr. Nance continued to build on the foundation laid by his predecessors. Off campus, Nance was very involved in the social and political affairs of South Carolina. He was an active participant in the Democratic Party, and at one state convention he served as president. He lobbied the General Assembly and began to secure funds previously unavailable to the college. He secured funding for the Smith-Hammond-Middleton Memorial Center and a health and physical education building, added to the Hodge Hall Science Building and made additions to the Kirkland W. Green Student Center, housing for married students, Soujourner Truth Hall, the Women's Residence Hall, the Dr. Martin Luther King Auditorium, the I.P. Stanback Museum and Planetarium and the School of Business complex.

On July 1, 1986, upon Dr. Nance's retirement, Dr. Albert E. Smith became the sixth president of South Carolina State University. During

Smith's tenure, the college established working relationships with several major corporations, including Westinghouse, Hughes Aircraft, AT&T and Zerox. Ground was broken for a new women's dormitory in 1991. President Smith was instrumental in gaining university status for the college.

On January 13, 1992, the board of trustees named Carl A. Carpenter interim president. During his tenure, the new master plan for facilities was finalized, and approval was given for the construction of the fine arts building. There were improvements on Oliver C. Dawson Stadium, expansion of the 1890 research facilities and a new conference center at Camp Harry Daniels. The master's of arts teaching degree was approved by the South Carolina Commission on Higher Education, and accreditation visits for engineering technology and social work were conducted. The institution was designated South Carolina State University on February 26, 1992.

On September 30, 1992, the board of trustees named Dr. Barbara R. Hatton the first woman to assume the presidency of the SCSU, and she began her duties on January 4, 1993. During her tenure, she was instrumental in converting Felton Lab School into a state-of-the-art development school. Legislation was passed by the General Assembly allowing engineering tech students to sit for the engineering license examination in South Carolina. The new Oliver C. Dawson Bulldog Stadium and student center complex was completed.

On April 10, 1996, Dr. Leroy Davis was named the eighth president of South Carolina State. President Davis established the Center for Excellency in Transportation and Leadership. In December 2000, the university's accreditation was reaffirmed by the SACS. In 2001 the School of Business was accredited. The office of environmental health was established, Dukes Gymnasium was reopened and the "State" room was opened at the Columbia Airport.

On July 1, 2002, the board named retired chief justice Ernest A. Finney Jr. interim president. During his tenure, the Nuclear Engineering Program was approved by the South Carolina Commission on Higher Education. The program is a joint one with the University of Wisconsin; it is the only undergraduate nuclear engineering program at an HBCU and the first of its kind started in the nation. A $9 million grant was received to start up the Transportation Research Facility.

Dr. Andrew Hugine Jr. was named the ninth president of South Carolina State on May 16, 2003. President Hugine developed an Alumni Heritage Endowment Fund to allow the university a way to create perpetual funding for scholarships, capital improvements and endowed chairs. Under Hugine's leadership, an agreement with the University of South Carolina launched a faculty/student exchange program in nuclear engineering. Other accomplishments during his presidency included the computer science program, and a new master's of business administration degree in agriculture entrepreneurship was added to the curriculum. The largest number of new students enrolled in the history of the college occurred on his watch. He established the University Board of Visitors.

The ROTC program at South Carolina State was started in 1947. The first graduating class in 1948 consisted of six cadets. Five received regular army commissions, and one received a reserve commission. Since 1948, over 2,034 students have been commissioned to serve in the armed forces of this country as of May 2010.

From 1947 to 1968, enrollment in the ROTC program was mandatory for all able-bodied freshman and sophomore male students. A cross-enrollment program was initiated in 1968 to permit students from other local colleges, which did not have ROTC, to receive training at South Carolina State without having to transfer from their institutions. Today, there are cross-enrollment agreements with Claflin, Voorhees, Denmark TEC and Orangeburg TEC.

During the school year 1972–73, the Department of the Army initiated on a trial basis a five-year program of enrolling women in the ROTC program. South Carolina State was one of the ten states selected nationwide to participate in this program. The first female graduated in 1976. Since the program started, South Carolina State has commissioned over 206 females. The nickname for the South Carolina State ROTC is "Bulldog Battalion."

In many quarters, the South Carolina State ROTC program is referred to as "West Point South" because of the many officers it has produced. As of 2010, some fourteen state graduates have risen to the rank of general officer in the U.S. military.

General Colin Powell was the 2011 commencement speaker. He came because his mentor, General George Price of the South Carolina State ROTC class of 1951, asked him to attend and speak.

28

THE OLD BLACK HIGH SCHOOLS

During the time of segregation in South Carolina prior to 1954, the black high school principal was a powerful figure in the black community. Next to the black preacher, he was perhaps the most powerful and respected. Sometimes he wore both hats—preacher and principal. After 1969, this status would change. Black male principals became an almost endangered species as schools integrated and made adjustments. Some of these principals became assistant superintendents with limited authority. Some passed out supplies. Others directed the bus transportation of the students. Some took jobs with the newly created federal Opportunity Economic Organization and became directors of Community Action Agencies. With their departure, discipline began to decline in the schools.

Black principals were stern disciplinarians. It is said that all one of these men had to do was stand at one end of the hallway and clear his throat, and noisy students would scatter like roaches running into holes. There was no talking back to a principal or teacher and no cursing or smoking cigarettes. If one was punished for some infraction by the principal or teacher and the word reached his or her parents, a whipping would be waiting at home. Many could not figure out how parents got the word so fast about punishment at school. There were very few telephones in those days, but parents had a communication system that rivals today's Internet.

While the black principal was keeping order, the black teacher was doing a masterful job, with fewer resources and equipment than her white counterpart, imparting knowledge to her charges. Often times, she had more formal training than her white counterpart. Unable to attend

Clemson or USC for graduate studies because of segregation, she would go to Columbia University, New York University, Temple, Pittsburg or Atlanta University for advanced degrees. A Sumter teacher at Lincoln High School, Dr. Agnes H. Wilson, taught French and journalism. She had studied at the Sorbonne in Paris.

It was not unusual for a black teacher to spend the summer sleeping on cousin Bertha's living room couch in New York or Philadelphia while studying for a master's degree in education. Atlanta University was a haven for black teachers who sought master's degrees in library science. Located in Atlanta, Georgia, for years it was the only HBCU that offered a master's in most disciplines. Many of the black teachers of the 1940s and '50s held advance degrees from Atlanta University. Integration almost put Atlanta University out of business. Were it not for Carl Ware, Eldridge W. McMillan and Marvin S. Arrington, all members of the board of trustees at Clark College at that time, who strenuously argued and convinced fellow board members to bring Atlanta University into the fold of Clark College, the school would have closed. Had Atlanta University closed, the legacy of W.E.B. DuBois, John Hope and Horace Mann Bond, all icons of education at the school, would have been lost. In 1988, the boards of both institutions voted to consolidate, and Clark Atlanta University was born. Today, it is the largest of the private HBCUs and the only one to offer terminal degrees in most disciplines except law and medicine.

Today, there are only four of the old black high schools that are still active and in service as high schools. There is Burke High in Charleston, C.A. Johnson High in Columbia, Wilkinson High in Orangeburg and Wilson High in Florence. The others—at least, those that have not been victims to the wrecking ball—are either middle schools or have been converted to community centers for community activities.

Some of those buildings that are still around include Lincoln High in Sumter, which is being used for community purposes. Lincoln dates back to 1874 and is possibly the oldest of the black high schools. One of its early principals was Johnson C. Whittaker of Camden, who came to Sumter after marrying the daughter of Sumter's first black physician, Dr. C.W. Birnie. This is the same Whittaker who was the second black to attend West Point (discussed in an earlier chapter). The Lincoln property sits on six acres of land in downtown Sumter. After integration, the school board built a mega high school, and the Lincoln building changed hands several times. The Catholic parish used it for a high school at one time. The school board used it for all tenth graders at one point. Trinity United Methodist bought the property. In 2008, the alumni of Lincoln, scattered over the country, purchased the property from Trinity. Currently, the Lincoln Center houses the Salvation Army's Boys and Girls Club, a United Way Project, the Sumter Academy, the Methodist Shepherd Center and the Lincoln Alumni Office. The Lincoln Alumni Office is in the process of renovating portions of the building to house a museum for black history and artifacts. Each year, the alumni sponsor a Legacy Keepers Gala on the Friday after Thanksgiving. Proceeds from this affair help reduce the mortgage on the building. The property is appraised at over $6 million.

Avery Institute in Charleston merged with the College of Charleston and has become the Avery Research Center for African American History and Culture. Avery's archive is the collection point for the papers of many African Americans in South Carolina. Avery maintains several galleries and other spaces. It sponsors exhibitions. It houses permanent displays and is a site for lectures, poetry readings, book signings, jazz performances and art exhibitions throughout the year.

On the eastern edge of Sumter County, there is the Goodwill Parochial School, which was founded by the Presbyterian Church to educate newly freed slaves. The alumni organized and restored that school building. It is now a museum and historical site. Some of its supporters include Clifton Davis, the actor in the TV series *Amen*, and Anna Maria Hosford, who starred with him. They have been part of fundraising efforts for the Goodwill School.

The old Dennis High School building in Bishopville has been acquired by the alumni, and it now serves as the Dennis Community Center. Major renovations to the center began in 2009 with the help of state senator Gerald Malloy of Hartsville. He was able to secure some funds from the General Assembly to begin that restoration and renovation. Dennis was the only high school for blacks in the county until Mount Pleasant High was built in the 1950s.

Up in Greenwood, the home of the old Brewer High School, some significant things have taken place. Greenwood County is the home of Dr. Benjamin E. Mays. With the leadership of Dr. Joseph D. Patton III, part of the Brewer campus has become the home of the Benjamin E. Mays Historical Preservation Site. On Tuesday, April 26, 2011, there was a dedication service. The birth house of Dr. Mays, the school he attended and a museum have all been relocated to the site. It was a great ceremony, and people turned out from all over the United States. Among the program's participants was Dr. Samuel DuBois Cook, president emeritus of Dillard

University; he eulogized Dr. Mays and shared personal reflections. There were also reflections by Billye Aaron, wife of baseball great Hank Aaron; Dr. Johnny McFadden of USC; and state senator Floyd Nicholson. Ambassador Andrew Young delivered the keynote address.

The Brewer High School building is also the home of the GLEAMNS Human Resources Commission, Inc. This agency is one of the oldest Community Action Agencies in the country, and Joe Patton is the CEO/director.

Over in Edgefield County, the home of Senator Strom Thurmond, there is Bettis Academy, which opened its doors on January 1, 1882. A Baptist minister, Alexander Bettis established the academy. The school had a commodity card stipulating the kinds and amounts of farm-raised produce parents could bring to the school in lieu of cash to pay for room and board. This method afforded many students, whose parents were poor, the opportunity to attend the academy. In 1933, the academy was accredited as a junior college. When it closed in 1952, the campus contained fourteen major buildings on 350 acres. Among the buildings still standing is the Bettis Library, where collections of documents recording the history of the school are housed. There is a group called the Bettis Academy Heritage Team whose goal is to collect, organize, preserve and display information relating to the history of the school.

In Chester County, there was Brainerd Institute, a school founded by the Presbyterian Church North following the Civil War to educate newly freed slaves in that area. The school closed in 1939. One of the last graduates was Vivian Ayers. Mrs. Ayers is the mother of two well-known actresses, Phylicia Rashad of *The Cosby Show* and Debbie Allen of *Fame*. The property fell into disrepair. The sisters purchased it and are in the process of renovating it on behalf of their mother. When it is completed, it will house a museum and theater complex. Vivian Ayers is the older sister of Bessie Ayers Moody-Lawrence, who served in the South Carolina House of Representatives until 2008. Bessie was the wife of Lindberg Moody, the outstanding basketball player at Lincoln High School in Sumter and at South Carolina State College. He died in an auto accident in 1975.

Penn School on St. Helena Island in Beaufort County is one of the nation's most historical and cultural institutions. It began in 1862 as an experiment to educate the island's newly freed slaves. It is the oldest and most persistent survivor of the Port Royal Experiment. It ceased to be a school in 1947, when the county took over the responsibility for educating black children. It was then converted into a conference center. It was the only place in

South Carolina and the South where black and white people could meet, eat together and sleep in the same buildings.

Penn became the retreat for Dr. Martin L. King; there, he planned and strategized his activities and enjoyed rest and relaxation. During the 1960s, it was a training place for Peace Corp volunteers. It also was a designated site for conscientious objectors to serve their alternate time instead of serving in the active military. Today, Penn continues to host conferences and meetings. John Gadson of Beaufort was the first person of color to serve as executive director of Penn. He followed Courtney Siceloff, who served for many years.

Booker T. Washington High School in Columbia was the last of the major black high schools to close in 1974. Over three thousand former students and faculty converged on the Township Auditorium on June 2, 1974, to witness a rededication of the Booker T. Washington ideals. Principal Harry B. Rutherford Sr., who served the school for over fifty years, in a moving and emotional plea, urged the audience to cooperate with alumni and a new foundation that was being established. Booker T. Washington was on property adjacent to the University of South Carolina. USC needed space for expansion, and the school was in the way. The school was closed, and USC took over the property. Today, there is a monument on the site to let the casual visitor know that once there was a high school here named Booker T. Washington. Others on program that day were Dr. Tom Jones, president of USC; Senator Hyman Rubin; Dr. William Lindler, superintendent of School District 1; and Hays Mizzell, school board member.

A physical reminder of BTW High School can be found today at 6509 North Main Street in Columbia. It shares the site with the Monteith Cultural Center. The building that houses the center is the former Monteith School building; it was relocated to that site, and it bears the name Booker T. Washington/Monteith Cultural Center. The Monteith name is from the Modjeska Monteith Simkins family. This is the school she attended, and her mother was the principal. The building fell into disrepair. It was relocated and renovated, and now it is what it is.

Another of the old schools is Howard Junior High in Prosperity, Newberry County. It is one of the few Rosenwald schools still standing. Bishop Fred C. James of the AME Church is a graduate of the school, and he is leading efforts to renovate and restore the old building. The Rosenwald comes from Julius Rosenwald, chairman of Sears Roebuck, who at the turn of the century in 1900 contributed funds to build or assist in the building of some five thousand schools for blacks in the South. These schools are referred to as "Rosenwald schools." A valuable portrait of Julius Rosenwald has been donated to the Lincoln High School Alumni Association, and it will be hung in the Alumni Museum when it is completed.

Up in Oconee County, there is the Seneca Institute. It was founded as a Christian primary and secondary school for blacks in 1899 by the Seneca River Baptist Association. The first principal was Dr. John Jacob Starks. He served for thirteen years and left to become president of Morris College in Sumter. The Seneca Institute became Seneca Junior College in 1926. In 1978, the Seneca River Improvement Association dedicated the Seneca Institute Family Life Center, a multipurpose building, as a community center. It is located on the old campus of the Seneca Institute.

In Camden, South Carolina, there was a school named the Boylan-Haven-Mather Academy. It operated from 1897 to 1983. The academy began as three private boarding schools that eventually merged into one. All three of these schools were founded by the Women's Home Missionary Society of the Methodist Episcopal Church in the late 1800s to educate the children of former slaves. First, there was the Boylan School in Jacksonville, Florida; the Haven School in Savannah, Georgia; and Mather Academy in Camden, South Carolina. In 1959, the three schools merged. In 1983, the Methodist Women Division of the United Methodist Church closed the school because of new mission priorities, rising costs and declining enrollment brought on by integration. The Women's Mission ordered the buildings torn down in 1995 and sold part of the land for commercial use. There is a marker on the original site indicating that Mather was there. Several of Mather's outstanding graduates include John Roy Harper II, who served as the NAACP general counsel, and Congressman James E. Clyburn. Clyburn spent eleven years at Lincoln High in Sumter, but his senior year was spent at Mather; therefore, he is technically a Mather graduate.

Up in the northeast part of South Carolina, in Chesterfield County, there is the Coulter Memorial Academy site in the town of Cheraw. Coulter was a boarding school for boys and girls founded by the Negro Presbyterian Church USA. The founder was Reverend J.P. Crawford, with support from Mrs. C.E. Coulter, from whom the school received its name. The Reverend G.W. Long was the principal of Coulter from 1908 until 1943, when it became a junior college. It closed in 1947, when the public school system took over educating all of the children in the county. On the site of the campus, there is still the George W. Long Presbyterian Church building and the main academic building. A historical marker preserves the site. At one time, as many as 510 students attended Coulter, and they came from both North and South Carolina. Dr. G.W. Long, the longtime principal, attended Brainerd Institute in Chester and graduated from Biddle University, which is now Johnson C. Smith University in Charlotte, North Carolina. There is a national alumni association of Coulter, and it has periodic meetings in Cheraw.

29

ECONOMIC PARTICIPATION

In many communities, there was a black business district. In Sumter, it was Manning Avenue. In Columbia, it was Washington Street. In Spartanburg, it was South Liberty Street. In Greenville, it was East McBee and Fall Street. In Florence, it was Dargan Street. In Charleston, it was Spring Street. In these districts, one could find a drugstore, doctors' and dentists' offices, an insurance company (North Carolina Mutual and/or Pilgrim Health and Life), a grocery store, a dry cleaners, restaurants and a dry goods store. Today, most of these businesses do not exist. There are those who say integration caused the demise of many of these neighborhood businesses. Urban renewal hastened the process.

In the days prior to 1970, when white financial institutions would not grant credit to persons of color, one could go to Victory Savings Bank in Columbia to get financing for an automobile or a mortgage for a home. Also, the insurance companies, North Carolina Mutual and Pilgrim Health and Life, provided direct mortgages for homes. In Columbia, there was Richland County Council Federal Credit Union, which provided financing for black teachers. On John's Island in Charleston County, there was a credit union founded by Easu Jenkins for black farmers. In Florence, Trinity Baptist Church operated a credit union to serve that community. Brookland Baptist Church operates a full-service credit union in West Columbia.

In 1972, James Hopkins, Priscilla F. Murrell and James L. Felder were able to get a license to open and operate the first black-owned consumer finance company in Columbia. The name was Carolina Finance Corporation, and it operated on Farrow Road. Hopkins owned an appliance store on

Colonel Drive in Columbia and was having difficulty getting financing for his customers. Carolina Finance was the answer to that problem.

Victory Savings Bank was replaced when a group of black investors, headed by Dr. David Swinton of Benedict College and Charles Gary, a local realtor, purchased its assets and opened a new bank, South Carolina Community Bank. In addition to the headquarters office and a branch in Columbia, there are branches in Sumter, Eastover and Orangeburg. Clente Flemming, a retired Bank of America officer, serves as president.

In retail sales, Leevy's Department Store on Assembly Street in Columbia could compete with Tapps Department Store. The business dated back to 1922 and was the brainchild of Isaac S. Leevy and family (this is the same Leevy's Funeral Home family). In the 1970s, Fashions Unlimited, a men's store, opened on Main Street in Columbia selling the latest in men's high fashion.

In 1983, Associated Office Products, a company that sold office supplies and equipment, was founded by Willie Scott and James L. Felder and operated on North Main Street. It was later replaced by JON-KER, Inc., which was founded by Perry and Barbara Jones. It continues to operate in 2011.

In most black communities, there was a black-owned food store. In Columbia, Ron Staley owned P-Mart on Taylor Street next to Allen University's Hurst Football Stadium. The Baxely family in Columbia operated several neighborhood food stores. They are all closed now. Allen University got into the food business when it opened a shopping center on Taylor Street that was anchored by Food Lion.

Prior to 1970, there were seventeen drugstores in South Carolina owned by black pharmacists. Today, there are only two, Jamison Pharmacy in Orangeburg and Finklin Medicine Shoppe in Columbia. In 1998, Lance Wright of Columbia (my son-in-law) founded National Direct Home Pharmacy. This is a mail-order pharmacy that serves over ten thousand patients per month with all of their drug needs. Additionally, National Direct has a sales force in North Carolina and Georgia that markets diabetic supplies. At its peak, the company counted over one hundred employees. Wright also provides hospice services through his company, AHAVA Hospice.

There were seven full-service hospitals serving the black community prior to 1970. They were Good Samaritan in Columbia, Community Hospital in Sumter, McClellan Banks in Charleston, Bulls Clinic in Spartanburg, Benevolent Society in Kingstree, Taylor Lane Hospital in Columbia and

Peoples Hospital in Newberry. They no longer exist. However, a new health provider, called Community Health Centers, has replaced these old hospitals. The first of these centers was founded in Beaufort County, the Sea Island Comprehensive Health Center. Tom Barnwell of Hilton Head Island was the moving force in this development. In later years, Wallace Brown of Columbia headed health centers in Richland County.

In the construction industry, one could always find a local homebuilder, and sometimes he could build a church. There were two large construction companies in the state. One was Langley Construction Company in Columbia. Langley's motto was: "We build everything from a chicken coop to a motel." In Charleston, it was H.A. DeCosta Company. His company was named *Black Enterprise* magazine's top black businesses in the United States in 1977 and 1978. In Sumter, Neal Brothers was the top builder and continues in the business today.

The new construction companies on the block today include Construction Dynamics, Inc., founded by Nate Spells in 1987. This Clemson graduate builds schools and churches all over South Carolina and in the Southeast. DESA, Inc, a company founded by Diane E. Sumpter, does construction management. She also provides consultant services to minority businesses on a variety of issues. Enviro Ag Science, Inc., a company founded by Dr. Louis B. Lynn, does construction, landscaping and related work. Lynn, who was in the second black graduating class at Clemson, holds a PhD and is the only black serving on the board of trustees at Clemson.

In road construction, Taylor Brothers, Inc., of Columbia works on projects in South Carolina and the Southeast. The Jackson Brothers of Columbia handles a lot of roadwork, as well.

In manufacturing, there were four companies that made clothing. Sometimes these companies were referred to as "cut-and-sew operations." In Pageland, South Carolina, there was the Pageland Manufacturing Corporation owned by Charles Brewer with forty-plus employees. In Conway, there were two cut-and-sew operations owned by black families. In Bishopville, a team of investors that included Dr. O.R. Ruben of Morris College, Ruben Gray, Dr. Claude Stevenson, Billie S. Fleming, William Dannelly, Wilbur L. Jeffcoat, James Davis and James L. Felder founded the Bishop Mills Sewing Plant. At one point, it was the second-largest employer in Lee County with a workforce of one hundred employees running two shifts. This was during 1969–70, when the hottest style for ladies was hot pants. The plant turned out tens of thousands of them. It made children's clothes, as well. Priscilla Reid Hammond of Camden was plant manager.

In Charleston, a former schoolteacher, W. Melvin Brown, founded the American Development Corporation. At its peak, he employed 350 people to make products for the U.S. Department of Defense. His business made the list of *Black Enterprise*'s 100 Top Businesses in 1977–79. He was grossing over $20 million a year. Following his death, the business was sold.

The Shumpert family in Columbia manufactured lumber and wood products for homebuilding and commercial use until 2008. Gloria Shumpert James, third generation of Shumperts and her husband, Marshall James, were the last to operate the business before closing it.

In the 1970s, blacks began to get more involved in real estate and insurance sales. In Columbia, there were Abraham & Ruff, Willie Williams & Associates and Capital City Real Estate & Insurance. In Orangeburg, two companies, Middleton Real Estate & Insurance and Montgomery Real Estate & Insurance, served the needs of the black communities and others. In Sumter, Charles Riley operated Avenue Realty, and Bob Palmer owned Guaranty Insurance Agency. In Charleston, J. Arthur Brown was the realtor.

Prior to the 1964 Civil Rights Act, blacks could not stay at white-owned hotels and motels. However, there were black-owned facilities. In Columbia, there were the Town 'n' Tourist Motel and Carolina Motel. There was the Ghana Motel in Greenville, Brooks Motel in Charleston, Bennett's Motel in Florence and the Gordon Hotel on Atlantic Beach.

On the coast of South Carolina, there were always black fishermen hooking fish for a living in their small boats. In 1968, a group of fishermen, led by Tom Barnwell and David Jones of Hilton Head Island, organized the Hilton Head Fishing Coop. They owned ten shrimp boats and leased space to others who wanted to use their dock. It was not unusual to see a line of refrigerated trucks waiting for the boats to come in with the day's catch. The coop faded away in the early 1990s.

This new generation of black entrepreneurs steered away from the mom-and-pop businesses and went the franchise route. Since 1980, in Columbia, Charleston, Sumter, Greenville and other cities, one will find major franchises owned by individuals and families. In Columbia, the Langleys own several McDonald's. Alex English, the star basketball player at USC and in the NBA, and his wife own several Wendy's franchises. Sidney B. Fulton of West Columbia owns several Popeye restaurants. Michael McNeil owns two Subway locations. Sam Glover and the late Stevie Stephenson owned Burger Kings at one time.

There was always a local restaurant in the black community, oftentimes specializing in fish. In Columbia today, Frank and Millie Houston have taken the restaurant business to a new level from what it was in the old days. Not only does this couple operate a successful catering business, Houston Catering, but they also operate Houston's Low Country Grille on North Main Street. The restaurant has a very diverse customer base who visits regularly.

The black church has been a mainstay in the black community. In effect, it has been the glue that has held many communities together. In recent years, in addition to saving souls, the church has become an economic engine. Brookland Baptist Church in West Columbia, where the Reverend Charles B. Jackson Sr. is shepherd of the flock, in addition to running a full-service credit union, the church operates a banquet and convention center that is booked year-round for meetings and conferences. At lunch time on any given day, the dining area is packed with blacks and whites enjoying one of the best buffets in Columbia.

Not to be outdone by Brookland, Bible Way Church of Atlas Road is planning a shopping center and single-family homes and owns most of the property on both sides of Atlas Road from Bluff Road to Shop Road. Bible Way was founded by Bishop A.C. Jackson. He started out in a storefront building, and upon his passing, he left to his sons, Darrell, Randal and Rodrick, a multimillion-dollar complex and a congregation of over five thousand members.

The Presbyterian Church USA sent Reverend Richard Bozier to Columbia in 1970 to organize a new church there. The Greenview section of Columbia was chosen as the site for the new church. It was named Northminster. Dozier, a native of Saluda, was also given the responsibility of overseeing the building of a new residential community in the Harbison area of Columbia, where the Presbyterian Church owned hundreds of acres of land. The Harbison Development Corporation was formed, and Dozier chaired the board. Fred A. Johnson of Atlanta was brought in to ramrod the project, and Jasper M. Cureton, later Judge Cureton, did most of the early legal work for the project. Hundreds of homes were built in Harbison. It was the beginning of the development in that area.

First Nazareth Baptist Church is the third of the three mega black churches in Columbia. It operates a large child development center at 2351 Gervais Street. Reverend Blakely N. Scott is the pastor of this church, which has had a member of the Neal family serving its members for the past seventy-plus years. Scott's uncle, Reverend W.H. Neal, served the church prior to passing it on to him.

In Sumter, Mount Pisgah AME Church was the first religious entity to sponsor an apartment complex in 1968 under the leadership of Bishop Fred C. James.

In Georgetown, Bethel AME Church owns a thirty-nine-unit affordable housing complex. In September 2010, Bethel purchased an eighty-nine-unit motel on Highway 17. Bethel is the home church of first lady Michelle Obama's grandparents. She spoke at the church during the 2008 presidential campaign.

30

BLACK NEWSPAPERS, RADIO AND TV STATIONS

B lack newspapers are more than a business; they are an institution. Before radio, television and the Internet, black newspapers were the primary source of news for the black community. For over 176 years, they told the world that black people do exist, they are educated, they fought to maintain the freedom that this country has enjoyed and they invented things that have made all of America healthier. Black newspapers date back to the time of Frederick Douglass, when he first published the *North Star.*

In South Carolina, the early newspapers date to 1931, when John H. McCray of Charleston published the *Lighthouse* and attorney Earl A. Parker of Sumter published the *Informer.* These two papers merged in 1941 and became the *Lighthouse & Informer.* McCray moved the paper to Columbia. It became the voice of the NAACP and its legal struggles during the 1940s and '50s.

In the early 1960s, Nathaniel Abraham Sr. of Orangeburg moved to Columbia and began publishing newspapers that continue today with his son at the helm. The current publication is the *Carolina Panorama*, based in Columbia.

In 1970, a second paper, *Black News*, surfaced in Columbia, published by Isaac Washington and Redfern II. The paper grew and became the *South Carolina Black Media Group*, offering satellite editions in various communities around the state.

A third paper hit the streets of Columbia in 1971. It was the *Palmetto Post.* The founders of this paper included Zack Weston, Dewey M. Duckett Jr., Laura E. Lilliewood, John Goodwin and James Hopkins. The paper lasted for five years.

The fourth paper that would appear in Columbia in 1993 was the *Carolina Tribune*. It was founded by James Redfern II. At this point, he had severed his relationship with *Black News*. He could not get publishing out of his system, so he started this new paper.

In Charleston, Jim French, a navy veteran, began publishing the *Chronicle*, which has been running for over thirty years. In the 1980s, a second paper appeared in Charleston, the *Coastal Times*, founded by Jim Clyburn and managed by his daughter, Mignon.

In the Pee Dee area of the state—Darlington, Florence, Dillon and Marion Counties—Larry Smith publishes a string of papers out of his company, the Pee Dee Group.

In the early 1970s, *Focus News* was founded in Greenville. It no longer exists.

Many local community newspapers would surface and fade away. Today, the *Chronicle*, *Black News*, the Pee Dee Group and *Carolina Panorama* are still in business.

The trade association for black publishers is the National Newspaper Publisher Association (NNPA). The organization has been around for seventy-two years. It has weathered good times and bad but is still a force to be reckoned with.

PRIOR TO 1954, THERE WERE no black-owned radio stations in South Carolina. There was only one in the entire country, and that was WERD in Atlanta, owned and operated by Jesse B. Blayton. It went on the air in 1953. In many communities, white owners of radio stations would allow time for black participation on Sunday mornings. Usually, there would be gospel quartets singing live in the studio. Some evening programs would feature gospel programs.

In 1956, in Sumter, radio station WSSC allowed the Lincoln High School *Echo* newspaper staff a thirty-minute program once a week to report on the activities of the school. Two of the persons reporting those activities were Winifred Gadson and James L. Felder. In the afternoon on the same station, one hour was allowed for playing "black music." Sumter's first black deejay was Joe Anderson. He was an army officer veteran, and his mother, Mrs. Hallie Pratt, taught in the school system of Sumter. His radio handle was "Jiving Joe."

In Columbia in 1954, WOIC radio station allowed Reverend William McKinley Bowman to come aboard and play gospel songs. Later, Reverend Bowman became a partner and part owner of the station. Whites owned controlling interest in the station until 1974, when a group of black investors purchased the station. The group included I.S. Leevy Johnson, J. Wade Degraffenreid, Elliott E. Franks III and Harry B. Rutherford Jr. They formed a company and named it Nuance Corporation. Franks, who was secretary of the corporation, was named general manager to handle the day-to-day operations. The station became a forum for many radio personalities that included Ethel Taylor, Bill Terrell, Lou Summers, Jesse Bower, Eugene Waiters and Don Frierson, to name a few. The station was sold to a group of white investors for a time. In early 2000, it was purchased by Inner City Broadcasting. Inner City is a New York company owned by the Sutton family, whose patriarch is the late Percy Sutton. Sutton, a black native from San Antonio, Texas, was part of the "Godfather Group" of Harlem that included Congressman Charlie Rangel, Basil Patterson and Adam Clayton Powell. They were the big four of Harlem's politics from 1950s until recently. In addition to WOIC, Inner City owns the following stations in Columbia: WHXY, ROCK 93, FOX 102.3, ESPN and WWDM.

In Charleston, WPAL radio station went on the air in the 1970s with a group headed by Bill Saunders and D. Ward Wilson. Today, it is still a functioning station.

In the early 1990s, Reverend Raleigh Williams of Walterboro received a license to put WTGH on the air in Cayce, South Carolina. Later, that station was purchased by Alex Snipes, who formed Glory Communications, Inc., and now has a string of stations located in Columbia, Florence, Orangeburg, St. Stephens and Sumter. The Columbia stations are WFMV, WGCV and WQXL. The Florence station is WPDT. In Orangeburg, it is WSPX. In St. Stephens, it is WTUA. In Sumter, it is WLJI. On WGCV in Columbia, which is 620 on the AM dial, Don Frierson hosts a daily program at noon known as *The Urban Scene*, and P.A. Bennett hosts an afternoon drive show that keeps the public informed on current events and community activities, discusses issues with guests and offers a "talk back" segment.

THERE IS ONE BLACK-OWNED TV station in South Carolina: WZRB, Channel 47, located in Columbia. It is owned by the Roberts Companies, a $30 billion corporation headquartered in St. Louis, Missouri. It owns hotels, resorts, retail centers and theaters throughout this country and the Caribbean. The black owners of this conglomerate are Steve and Michael Roberts, former members of the St. Louis City Council. They became entrepreneurs and never looked back.

From Peaceful Protests to Groundbreaking Rulings

PERIODICALLY, A BLACK MAGAZINE WILL surface for a period of time and fade away. Sometimes these publications publish monthly, bimonthly or twice a year. Eleven years ago, *Imara Magazine* for women started circulating and continued to be published bimonthly as of 2011. The magazine was founded by Wendy C. Brawley and her husband, Paul Brawley. The corporate name is Imara Communication Group, Inc. Wendy serves as CEO and publisher, and Paul is president and CFO. Paul is the elected auditor for Richland County. Wendy has served on Richland School Board 1. While this magazine is geared toward women, it also features articles on men. It is done very professionally and has a wide circulation in South Carolina.

In keeping up with the latest technology of the times, Calvin Reese, who published a small paper at one time, now has an online magazine that can be found at Millennium.com.

31

NONGOVERNMENT ORGANIZATIONS

While the NAACP, SCLC, VEP and SNCC worked to remove barriers of discrimination, there were nongovernment agencies that prepared blacks for entry into the workplace of these newfound opportunities.

The first of these agencies was the Greater Columbia Community Relations Council, which was formed in 1960 to better race relations in Columbia. It grew into an organization that trained blacks for white-color jobs in banks and retail stores. Milton Kimpson was the first director, followed by David Burton, Preston Winkler, Jesse Washington and Lee Cato. It continues today as part of the Greater Columbia Chamber of Commerce.

In 1967, the Urban League came to Columbia. The leaders who brought the league to Columbia included Anthony and Alice Hurley and Colonel Ordie P. Taylor. Its first executive director was Daisy D. Johnson. When Mrs. Johnson resigned to accept a position at South Carolina State College, she was replaced by Elliott E. Franks III. Franks resigned to become a part owner and manager of WIOC radio station. Hiram Spain replaced Franks. In 1984, James T. McLawhorn took the reins and has served continually since, as of this writing (2012). Other Urban Leagues have been opened in Greenville and Charleston. South Carolina Urban Leagues are affiliates of the National Urban League based in New York. There are over one hundred affiliates in the United States.

Founded in 1910, the mission of the Urban League is to enable blacks to secure economic self-reliance, parity, power and civil rights. In its 101-year history, the National Urban League has had only eight executive directors. Dr. George E. Hayes was the first, followed by Eugene Jones,

Lester Granger, Whitney Young, Vernon E. Jordan, John E. Jacobs, Hugh B. Price and Marc Morial.

The Opportunities Industrialization Center came to Columbia in 1972. OIC, as it is called, was founded by Reverend Leon Sullivan in Philadelphia as a manpower-training program. The person selected to head the center was Priscilla R. Hammond of Camden. Its early board of directors included Garnell McDonald, John H. Lumpkins Jr., Calvin Harris, Colonel Ordie P. Taylor, Leon Babridge and a young lawyer named Jean Toal, who would become chief justice of the South Carolina Supreme Court. Training was offered in typing, shorthand, cashier sales, on-the-job-training and construction and heavy equipment operation.

In 1964, President Lyndon Johnson pushed through Congress the Civil Rights Act of 1964. The act created an Office of Economic Opportunity to oversee a variety of community-based antipoverty programs. It authorized Community Action Agencies (CAP) to reduce the cause and conditions of poverty in a geographical area. The board of directors of these agencies must be composed of representatives from three community sectors: one-third low-income people, one-third private agencies and one-third public agencies. The agency's objective is to serve economically and socially disadvantaged individuals and families and enable them to become self-sufficient. This program provided opportunities for black men and women to manage and supervise blacks and whites in a position other than principal of an all-black school. Many blacks left teaching to work in these agencies.

There were several human rights organizations composed of blacks and whites that supported the struggle for civil rights in South Carolina. Alice Spearman headed the South Carolina Human Relations Council, an organization that worked for racial harmony in the state. She was vilified and attacked by the KKK and called "nigger lover." James McBride Dabbs of Rip Rap Plantation in Sumter County chaired the Southern Regional Council in Atlanta. The council was the regional organization that fostered better race relations throughout the South. He was a white target of the KKK. A. McKay Brabham, who edited the *Methodist Advocate*, constantly chastised the white power structure to treat blacks equally.

Other whites who worked openly to ease the tension of racism in South Carolina were Max Secrest, editor of the *Cheraw Chronicle*; Marion Wright of the Southern Regional Council; Barbara Sylvester of Florence; the late Joe Sapp of Columbia; John Bolt Culbertson of Greenville, the white lawyer who did not shy away from any legal matter that affected blacks; and Brett Bursey, a mentee of Modjeska Simkins. Husband and wife Don and Carole

Fowler, who both served as chairs of the South Carolina Democratic Party at different times, reached out to include blacks in all segments of the party. Charles T. "Bud" Firrello was an early force in assisting Jim Clyburn in the early days of his political career.

At Penn Center, on St. Helena Island, Courtney Siceloff opened the doors of Penn for meetings between blacks and whites when no other places were available. There were others.

A NOTE ON SOURCES

Many sources were utilized and consulted during the research and writing of this book, including the author's personal knowledge and involvement in the events covered, the Avery Research Center, interviews with 112 history makers and various newspaper accounts of the events.

ABOUT THE AUTHOR

James L. Felder has been involved in voter registration and education in South Carolina since 1967. He was one of three blacks elected to the South Carolina House of Representatives in 1970, becoming the first to serve since Reconstruction. His first book, *I Buried John F. Kennedy*, reveals the role he played in the funeral of President Kennedy in 1963. He lives in Columbia, South Carolina. He has two children, Jimmy and Adrienne, and two grandsons, Lance and Sean.

Visit us at
www.historypress.net